Early Settlers in the Borders

Scottish Borders Council
Department of Planning and Development

Scottish
Borders
C O U N C I L

First published 1997.
Department of Planning and Development, Scottish Borders Council.

A British Library Cataloguing-in-Publication Data record for this book is available from the British Library.

ISBN: 0 9530438 00

Designed by the Graphic Section,
Department of Planning and Development.
Printed and bound by Kelso Graphics, The Knowes, Kelso, Scotland TD5 7BH.

Early Settlers in the Borders

Foreword

It is a memorable experience to travel along a Border valley on a bright day in late winter. Traces of vanished ramparts and ditches, hut circles, roads, field rigs and cultivation terraces are thrown up by the oblique sunshine as lines of shadow on the green fields of the slope. Between the modern, obliterating cultivation of the valley floor and the tops of the hills, an ancient landscape is projected as an endless and varying show.

But how are we to understand it? What peoples drew these lines, and how long ago, and why? What was the environment like? What wild animals did they encounter? How did they farm? Who cleared off the original woodland cover? How was society organised? Was it warlike or peaceful? How did the ordinary people, the immediate ancestors of modern Borderers, actually live?

This excellent booklet will set you on the trail to answer all these questions, and will tell you where you can go if you want to see some of these sites at close quarters. As the authors observe, our forefathers were every bit as clever as we are. They had less technology, but they lived closer to nature. If you wish to meet them on their own ground, read this book and then visit Eildon Hill North, Edin's Hall Broch or Dreva Craig. Or stand before the Yarrow Stone, where a Dark Age inscription begins: 'This is the everlasting memorial'. The world which the authors begin to open for us, is the start of our world: it is, we can now understand, our own cradles that we see on the hillsides.

Christopher Smout
Historiographer Royal in Scotland and Director,
Institute for Environmental History,
University of St Andrews
Vice Chairman, Scottish Natural Heritage.

Acknowledgements

This booklet was written, compiled and edited by John Dent and Rory McDonald of the Archaeology and Countryside Section, and designed by the Graphics Section, in the Department of Planning and Development, Scottish Borders Council, as part of the "Heritage Interpretation Project".

Scottish Borders Council is pleased to acknowledge financial support from the European Regional Development Fund and Scottish Natural Heritage which assisted in the production of this book as part of the Heritage Interpretation Project.

We would like to thank the following people for their help and advice during the preparation of this booklet: Richard Allan, Chris Badenoch, David Breeze, Ian Brown, Rosamond Brown, Fiona Colton, Lesley Dorward, Doreen Grove, Derek Hall, Strat Halliday, Rosemary Hannay, John Harrison, Roger Hemming, Keith Robeson, Christopher Smout, Rob Threadgold and Richard Tipping

Scottish Borders Council wishes to thank Caledonian Newspapers Ltd., Colin Martin, Historic Scotland and the National Museums of Scotland for kind permission to reproduce those photographs and drawings indicated in the text.

Introduction

Although the border between Scotland and England runs from sea to sea, the historic counties of Roxburghshire, Berwickshire, Selkirkshire and Peeblesshire have long been identified as "the Borders", a perception which has been continued by the modern administrative areas of the former Borders Region, and its successor Scottish Borders. The special character of this area and its people owes much to frontier history, but this book examines the thousands of years of development which shaped the people and the landscape up to the formation of the early historic kingdoms.

How and where did people live? what stresses and strains did they encounter? how did they affect their environment? and when did these processes occur? are questions which we seek to answer in this book. We begin with an historical outline (Part 1) to explain the geography of the region and provide the chronological framework. In Part 2 we examine how the way of life changed with time, looking in turn at the basic requirements of food and shelter, at how society was organised, at the patterns of settlement which evolved, and finally at the rituals and contacts which were developed. The impact which all these had on the environment is examined in Part 3, and sites which illustrate the main stages of human settlement are described in Part 4. Terms which are printed in italics and may be unfamiliar are explained in the Glossary section at the end of the book.

One purpose of this book is to give Borderers and visitors a greater awareness of the rich early history of the region, and increased understanding of remains which they may encounter in the landscape. Please note, however, that mention of an archaeologically important site in the text does not indicate that it may be visited. The reader should be aware that although many sites are marked on Ordnance Survey maps or may be readily visible in the landscape, most are located on private land and are not generally accessible. At the end of the book, however, the reader will find a list of those sites which are open to the public at the time of printing, those museums which contain collections of artefacts, and sources of further information.

Please remember, whenever visiting these sites, always follow the Country Code:

- Guard against all risk of fire
- Fasten all gates
- Keep dogs under close control
- Keep to paths across farm land
- Avoid damaging fences
- Leave no litter
- Safeguard water supplies
- Protect wildlife, wild plants and trees
- Go carefully on country roads
- Respect the life of the countryside

Table of Contents

Early Settlers in the Borders

Part 1:

Historical Background

Time Chart

4,400 million years ago	The Earth forms and gradually cools, with an atmosphere and oceans over most of its surface.	
500 to 400 million years ago	In the *Iapetus* Ocean of the Southern Hemisphere the bodies of simple shell fish and other dead marine animals sink into sediments which are compressed by colliding continents and pushed up to form the Southern Uplands.	*Ordovician* and *Silurian* eras
400 million years ago	Volcanic activity associated with the closing of the *Iapetus* Ocean creates the rocks of the Pentland Hills, St Abb's Head and the Cheviot Hills.	*Devonian* era
370 million years ago	Primitive fish, amphibians and plants live in or beside lakes and lagoons, which fill with silt from adjacent barren deserts to form the Old Red Sandstone of the eastern Borders. These rocks lie unconformably over the weathered surface of earlier hills near Cockburnspath and at Jedburgh. During this period the Borders lie at a latitude of about 15° South.	
355 million years ago	Much of the land subsides beneath freshwater lagoons and quiet tropical seas; the Southern Uplands form islands adjacent to the land mass represented by the Scottish Highlands.	
350 million years ago	Buckling of the earth's crust causes volcanic activity in the form of vents and *dykes* which produce the rocks of the Kelso Traps, the Eildon Hills and Rubers Law.	
340 million years ago	Warm seas filled with coral reefs and marine life deposit muds which become limestones rich in fossils. Today these outcrop around West Linton and near the mouth of the Tweed.	*Carboniferous* era
330 million years ago	Around the shores of the Southern Uplands, a broad coastal plain threaded by river estuaries emerges from the sea and becomes covered with equatorial rain forest full of insects and inhabited by lizards. Invasion by the sea kills off the forest, but after the sea eventually withdraws the cycle begins again. Peat bogs formed by the forest fossilize into the coal seams of the Central Valley of Scotland (still worked at West Linton) and Northumberland.	
65 million years ago	Now lying in latitudes of about 48°N, the Borders have been dry land for about 280 million years ago, and subject to erosion as well as stresses which fracture the earth's crust and cause fault lines to fill with lava, forming basalt *dykes* near Hawick. This is the last phase of rock formation in the Borders.	*Tertiary* era

Fig.1 *Events in the formation and early settlement of the Borders.*

2 million years ago	Onset of arctic conditions covers the Borders with thick glaciers and ice sheets which round off valley sides and rock outcrops, and pulverise and transport rock fragments which are deposited when the ice thaws. This process is repeated many times as temperature patterns fluctuate.	*Pleistocene*
15,000 years ago	Melting ice leaves many *moraines*, *eskers* and *drumlins* exposed in a bleak *tundra* landscape.	
12,000 years ago	After a cooler interval, temperatures begin to rise again and mixed forest grows up over all but the highest peaks in the Borders. Hunter-gatherers occupy the forests and subsist on wild game and plants.	*Holocene/ Mesolithic*
9,000 years ago	A rise in sea level finally separates Britain from the European continent, halting natural colonisation by terrestrial animals and many plant species.	
6,000 years ago	Woodland clearance for agriculture begins, with introduction of farming methods and domesticated animal breeds, including sheep and goats.	*Neolithic*
4,500 years ago	Population growth, sustained by agriculture, leads to development of hierarchical *chiefdom* societies with individual burials and ceremonial monuments as expressions of personal prestige.	
4,000 years ago	Metalworking based on copper, in combination with tin to produce bronze, forms the basis of a new technology and encourages development of trading links.	*Bronze Age*
2,500 years ago	Unstable social conditions are represented by *hillforts* at a time when iron technology is expanding the available range of tools and weapons. In time conditions stabilize as strong leaders emerge and fortifications go out of use.	*Iron Age*
1,900 years ago	The first of a series of invasions by Roman troops manages to conquer the Borders for the province of Britannia, and establish occupying garrisons, which are pulled back to Hadrian's Wall in due course. This pattern continues into the 3rd century AD.	*Roman period*
1,400 years ago	Heathen Germanic settlers speaking Old English occupy the Tweed lowlands, which becomes part of the kingdom of *Northumbria*, but the upper Tweed remains part of the Christian British kingdom of *Strathclyde*, where Old Welsh is spoken.	*Dark Ages*

The Borders are situated in the Southern Uplands of Scotland and are mostly made up of the river system of the Tweed and its tributaries, which flow into the North Sea at Berwick upon Tweed, and the Liddle Water, which runs south and west into the Solway and the Irish Sea. The only lowland area is the Merse, the undulating plain of the lower Tweed which separates the Lammermuir Hills on the north from the Cheviot Hills to the south. Westwards, these uplands merge with the central massif of southern Scotland, reaching an altitude of 840m on Broad Law (*fig.2*).

This shape is the result of events which took place over hundreds of millions of years. In contrast, the history of human occupation of the Borders may be no more than half a million years and it is only during the last 12,000 that any tangible remains have been left for the archaeologist. This last period, in which more than 400 human generations were born, is the chief concern of this book, but some explanation of the structure of the Borders and how it came about is necessary first.

The Shape of the Borders

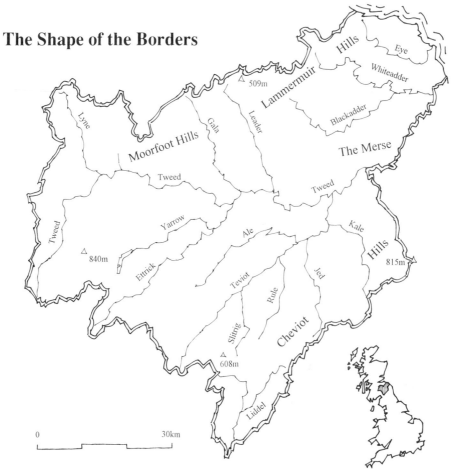

Fig.2 *Borders topography, drainage and location.*

Building the Borders

The Southern Uplands formed when two *tectonic plates* collided and pushed up the bed of an ancient ocean to form dry land. Such plates are large land masses which float on the molten *mantle* of the earth and move very slowly, causing *continental drift*. Where plates come together or drift apart the earth's crust is unstable and liable to earthquakes and volcanic activity. The ability of these plates to subside, uplift, fold and crack has led to the formation of a wide range of rock types, some of which were once molten (*igneous*) rocks, while other (*sedimentary*) rocks were deposited by wind or water.

The earliest rocks in the Borders were formed in the southern hemisphere between 500 and 400 million years ago, in the *Ordovician* and *Silurian* Periods, and were laid down as muddy sediments on the floor of the *Iapetus* Ocean at a time when life on earth consisted of primitive sea creatures. The fossilized remains of such creatures can be found in disused quarries in the western part of the region, where *graptolites* are the most common type (*fig.3*). These tiny extinct animals lived together in buoyant branching colonies in which each section was ridged like a saw blade.

Fossil Life Forms

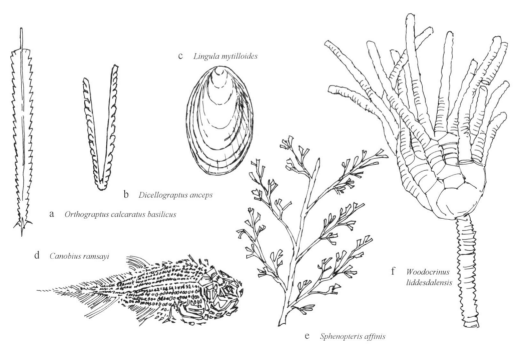

c   *Lingula mytilloides*

b   *Dicellograptus anceps*

a   *Orthograptus calcaratus basilicus*

d   *Canobius ramsayi*

f   *Woodocrinus liddesdalensis*

e   *Sphenopteris affinis*

Fig 3   *Early life forms represented by fossils from the Borders include such shellfish as graptolites (a, b), mussels (c) and crinoids (f); as well as larger fish (d), and plants (e). Not to scale.*

It was these thick beds of sediment which were folded, buckled, and thrust up out of the sea between 400 and 360 million years ago as the ocean bed was squeezed between two converging continental masses *(fig.4)*. The predominant north-east to south-west alignment of ridges over much of the region is a result of this process. This *Devonian* period saw a further process of sedimentation, particularly over the lower, eastern part of the region, where rivers washed rock from

Origins of the Borders
Geography 4.50 million years

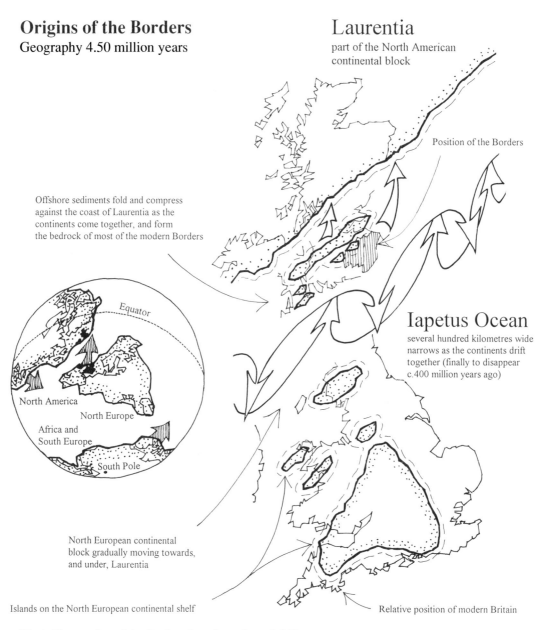

Laurentia
part of the North American continental block

Position of the Borders

Offshore sediments fold and compress against the coast of Laurentia as the continents come together, and form the bedrock of most of the modern Borders

Equator

North America

North Europe

Africa and
South Europe

South Pole

Iapetus Ocean
several hundred kilometres wide narrows as the continents drift together (finally to disappear c.400 million years ago)

North European continental block gradually moving towards, and under, Laurentia

Islands on the North European continental shelf

Relative position of modern Britain

Fig.4 *The creation of the Borders through continental drift.*

the eroding mountains into deltas and lakes to form Old Red Sandstone, a rock which is used extensively in buildings from Jedburgh to the coast. The junction between the base of the flat new *strata* (layers) and the folded and eroded surface of the old can be seen as *unconformities* at Jedburgh and Siccar Point (Cockburnspath). At this time the Borders were part of a large continent known as "*Laurentia*" which was made up of present day North America, Greenland and northern Europe. In the hot, wet climate of these times primitive fish lived in the shallow lakes, and some air-breathing varieties advanced as amphibians onto the land, where the first plants already grew. The buckling of the earth's crust (*faulting*) during this period caused molten rock to come to the surface as volcanic lava which cooled to form St Abbs Head (*Plate 1*) and the Cheviots.

After 345 million years ago the coast of "*Laurentia*" had receded to the edge of what is now the highlands of Scotland, but the Southern Uplands formed offshore islands, around which limestones formed in the shallow tropical seas. These rocks now outcrop around West Linton and near the mouth of the Tweed, and contain fossils of shellfish and corals. Fluctuations in sea level saw periodic silting up of coastal lagoons, and the growth of forests inhabited by the first lizards and insects. These forests were sealed beneath further marine sediments as the cycle continued and by 280 million years ago a whole

series of organic seams had formed which became the coal fields of the Central Valley of Scotland (still worked at West Linton) and Northumberland.

Further volcanic activity during this period created the Eildon and Minto Hills, Peniel Heugh, Dirrington Laws, the Dunion, Rubers Law and the "Kelso Traps", some of which represent the violent discharge of lava through volcanic vents (*Plate 2*). Elsewhere lavas seeped along rock seams to form the hard blisters or "*laccoliths*", or squeezed along *faulting* planes to form "*pipes*" and "*dykes*". The general shape of the Borders landscape was determined during this period.

The next 280 million years saw the emergence of dinosaurs (and their disappearance), and of birds and mammals. More *tectonic* activity detached Britain from North America and Greenland, and created the Atlantic Ocean. *Sedimentary* rocks continued to be laid down over what is now England, and Britain emerged as part of a Eurasian continental landmass.

During these aeons of time the future Britain moved on its *tectonic plate* from the southern hemisphere across the Equator and into northern latitudes. The final large scale geological change to affect the Borders began 2 million years ago, when the earth's climate grew colder and the northern hemisphere entered into the "Ice Age."

Climatic Changes and the Emergence of Britain

The period known as the "Ice Age" consisted of a series of cold phases, each of which lasted for tens of thousands of years, with shorter, warm intervals between. Some of the cold phases saw the growth of glaciers in the Borders hills, a fall in sea level which exposed the bed of the North Sea, and the advance of an ice sheet hundreds of metres thick southwards along the coasts of Britain *(fig.5)*.

From *corries* in the upper Tweed and on the Cheviot the glaciers moved mainly north-eastwards, picking up broken rocks and dragging them across the landscape, rounding off rock exposures, scouring and eroding the softer *strata*, and depositing sand, clay and other debris in sheltered places. Many of the north-south running valleys, such as that of the Eddleston Water have deposits of glacial boulders and clays on the west side, and oversteepened, ice-plucked slopes and thin soils on the east. In the eastern Borders prominent hills frequently have crag-and-tail formations, in which the south-western sides have been scoured by the ice and the slopes on the north-east are gentler.

As temperatures rose the glaciers retreated at differing rates, and meltwater could be held back by ice and ridges of rock, sand or clay before it was released to carve characteristic escape channels, good examples of which can be seen at Old Cambus (Cockburnspath), above Yetholm Loch, west of Carlops (West Linton), and at Grieston (Innerleithen). The material washed out by these streams or dropped by the melting ice altered the former drainage pattern by diverting watercourses, and creating numerous lochs and lochans in hollows, many of which have since filled up with silt and peat. The Whiteadder Water once flowed where the Billie Mire (Chirnside/Coldingham) lies today; the Kale Water used to flow eastwards to the Bowmont *via* Linton, instead of to the Teviot; and the Tweed, which now runs past Neidpath Castle (Peebles), formerly flowed *via* Manor and Cademuir.

During the last glaciation, the sea level was as much as 100m lower than today, due to the vast amounts of water locked up in ice sheets, and Britain was not an island, but a peninsula attached to the European continent. As the climate improved and the ice melted, the sea level began to rise once more, and *isostatic uplift* caused the central highlands of Scotland to rise as the colossal weight of ice diminished. This left many raised beaches and coastal platforms, particularly on the west coast and around the Firth of Forth. By c.6,500BC the North Sea and English Channel had re-formed, thereafter blocking any access to Britain except by sea, and temperatures reached their peak by c.4,000BC, when the British Isles enjoyed the warmest climate of the post-glacial period.

Britain during the last glaciation

Fig.5 *The British peninsula during the last glaciation, about 16,000 years ago.*

Hunters and Farmers

Our knowledge of events and processes in the history of human settlement of the Borders is derived almost entirely from archaeological study of sites and finds, for there are no written records before the early centuries AD. The period before that is "prehistoric".

The earliest human remains yet found in Britain (from Sussex) are half a million years old, and although we still await proof, there is no reason to suppose that hunter-gatherers did not penetrate the Borders long before the last glaciation. However, subsequent scouring of the landscape by ice is likely to have removed any camp sites which once existed.

The animals and plants which lived in the extensive forests which grew up over the British peninsula, eventually British Isles, provided food and raw materials for hunter-gatherers during the *mesolithic* period, which lasted from at least 10,000 to about 6,000 years ago and represents the final stage in Britain of a way of life which had supported humankind since its emergence. Sites in the Hebrides and Ireland show that these people had boats and may have been no more deterred from sea journeys than the hunting-gathering Esquimaux of Canada in recent years.

After Britain became an island, communication with the continent continued, and by this means cereal cultivation and sheep farming were introduced around 6,000 years (about 240 generations) ago. Agriculture supported a gradual rise in population, and this was accompanied by improvements in technology. Britain and the Borders were receptive to new ideas, and after about 2,500BC metalworking was practised, at first in copper and its alloys (especially bronze), and after c.650BC, in iron. These changes reflected a society which grew in extent and complexity as time passed.

By the 1st century AD (about 80 generations ago) the landscape and people were greatly changed from the time of the earliest farmers. There was still much woodland, but instead of the modest encroachment of early farmers, large areas had been cleared of trees for arable cultivation, even at high altitude. Settlements were numerous and a well-established network of trackways provided access through the remaining woodland and along and between the river valleys. The inhabitants enjoyed a better standard of living and by this time were organized into small kingdoms. Into this landscape came the first people to leave their names in the history books.

Roman Invasions

The written histories of Rome provide the first opportunity to identify actual people and events. They tell of the conquests of Julius Agricola, military governor of the Roman province of Britannia who led his armies beyond the Cheviot Hills and into what is now Scotland in c.AD78-79. His victories were followed up by the construction of forts and military roads, the chief of which ran from the legionary fortress at York to the northern frontier beyond the River Tay. In the AD120s the northern limit of the Roman Province was marked by Emperor Hadrian, who had a wall constructed to the south between the Tyne and Solway. In c.AD139-142 his successor Antoninus Pius pushed the frontier north to the Forth-Clyde line, and the Southern Uplands were once again incorporated into the Empire. By the later 2nd century Hadrian's Wall was once more the Roman frontier, although a further attempt to reconquer northern Britain was made by Emperor Septimius Severus in the early 3rd century.

The main Roman fort in the Borders was at *Trimontium* (Melrose), where the road from York crossed the Tweed (*fig.6*). The fort took its name, "Three Peaks" from the nearby Eildon Hills, and strategic reasons for its location probably included control of the large enclosure on North Hill, (Melrose), which has produced evidence of use at this time. The Latin sources which give us the name of *Trimontium* also tell us of two native peoples, the *Selgovae* and their neighbours, the *Votadini*, whose territories are generally considered to have included the Borders.

Fig.6 *The Roman military post of Trimontium at Newstead, looking east. Buried ditches, streets, wall foundations and other features had a visible effect upon growing corn during the dry summer of 1984. (photo: Colin Martin).*

Angles and Scots

In the 4th and 5th centuries AD, Europe saw the large scale movement of barbarian peoples, such as Vandals, Goths and Huns, which contributed to the collapse of the Roman Empire. In Roman Britain the withdrawal of the military government in c.AD410 led to the fragmentation of society and the emergence of a series of petty kingdoms. Beyond the Empire's northern frontier on Hadrian's Wall society had traditionally consisted of separate kingdoms, and it was pressure, particularly from the Picts (from beyond the Forth), apparently in league with migrant Scots (from Ireland) and Anglo-Saxons (from Denmark and Germany), which accelerated the collapse of Roman Britain and saw the establishment of new dynasties.

In the 5th and 6th centuries AD the British population of Southern Scotland came under increasing pressure from Gaelic-speaking Scots of *Dalriada* (Argyll) in the west and from English-speaking Angles of *Deira* and *Bernicia* (Yorkshire, Durham, and Northumberland) in the south. Advances by these neighbours were resisted, notably by warriors of the *Gododdin* (*Votadini*) who followed the former Roman road *Dere Street* from *Din Eiddyn* (Edinburgh) to their defeat at *Catraeth* (Catterick). Place names suggest that in the Borders the uplands of the west remained British, probably part of the kingdom of *Strathclyde*, and the arable lowlands of the east became part of Anglian *Bernicia* (*fig.17*).

Although other peoples were to influence the history and population of the Borders, by the end of the 7th century the main ethnic changes had taken place, the landscape had been largely opened up, and the basis of medieval and later rural settlement had been established.

Early Settlers in the Borders

Part 2:

Way of Life

Prehistoric and *Early Historic* peoples have bequeathed a rich heritage of archaeological clues from which, in the absence of their written testimony, it is possible to sketch out some of the problems they faced and how they solved them. People learned to minimise the risk of starvation and even provide a food surplus. They developed forms of transport and tools to make their life easier, and adapted their social organisation to suit an increased population. Many aspects of life changed with time, including religious beliefs, arts, and the relationships which groups of early settlers established with each other.

Basic Needs

It would be a great error to imagine that our prehistoric ancestors were less intelligent than their descendants today. The oldest tools were made at least two and a half million years ago, although their design improved only very slowly. People were more familiar with their environment than their modern counterparts and adapted a great range of naturally occurring resources to meet their needs, thereby ensuring that the race would survive for the future.

Food, clothing and shelter are the basic requirements for human survival. Tools to help provide these, and to make travel easier, were developed with time.

Food Supply

For over two million years humans relied on the productivity of the natural environment, even though climatic, seasonal, and environmental variation must have imposed severe strains and many must have perished from starvation. However, in the Borders no evidence has been found for human activity before the last glaciation, and only in the last 6,000

Fig.7 *Lochans and rivers attracted early settlers, who depended upon hunting for much of their food, until the introduction of farming c.6,000 years ago.*

Fig.8   *Mrs Anne Keddie with the skull of a 5,000 year old wild ox, or aurochs unearthed from a peat bog near Ashkirk in 1980. (photo: James Thomson).*

years have plants been grown and animals bred specifically to eat by the inhabitants.

Although many of the largest mammals, such as mammoths, bison and giant deer, were extinct by 9,000BC, potential game still included such *herbivores* as beaver, elk, red deer, wild horse, *aurochs* and wild boar, all of which were good to eat. Fish (including shellfish) and birds were also an important part of the diet, as may have been insects.   Predatory animals (*carnivores*), although generally poorer eating, would also be consumed when other game was not available.

Hunter-gatherers devised traps to help them catch their food, and hunted together, driving animals to places where they could be caught and killed using spears (*fig.7*).

In time they invented the bow so that they could wound and kill animals at longer range, and stone points for spears and arrows are some of the earliest tools which have survived in the Borders.

Plants were equally important sources of nourishment, but their availability is seriously affected by the seasons, and finds of hazelnut shells from Scottish sites suggest that people, like red squirrels, stored nuts for winter and spring. Our present native fruit and vegetables are descendants of ancient wild varieties, and then, as now, some must be eaten fresh while others can be stored. Although less common as a food today, seaweeds are available fresh all year round, and undoubtedly would have helped to sustain early peoples living close to the coast.

Plants can also be boiled, infused or fermented in water to provide pleasant drinks, many of which have medicinal properties.

Although the hunter-gatherer lifestyle was successful in satisfying basic needs, people sought to develop more effective ways of ensuring survival. The transition to farmer took place over a large area, and developed in the Middle East before people in Britain began to combine agriculture with hunting and gathering.

Fig.9 *Cereals were ground into flour using a stone quern; the flat saddle quern (left) of early farmers was superseded by the rotary quern (right) in the late 1st millennium BC.*

Early farmers may have caught and bred varieties of indigenous wild cattle (*Bos primigenius*) *(fig.8)* and pigs (*Sus scrofa*), and introduced domesticated strains of the Asiatic mouflon sheep (*Ovis orientalis*), and perhaps wild goat (*Capra aegagrus*). They also brought in forms of wheat developed from wild *einkorn* (*Triticum monococcoides*), and other domesticated grasses may have arrived as accidental

inclusions mixed among seed corn, clinging to clothing or stock, or even in animal droppings. By the 1st millennium BC at least ten varieties of cereals were available to British farmers, including forms of wheat (*Triticum* sp.), barley (*Hordeum* sp.), rye (*Secale cereale*) and perhaps oats (*Avena* sp.), while peas (*Pisum ativum*) and beans (*Vicia faba minor*) may also have been grown. Early farmers may have grown plants which we regard as weeds, such as Fat Hen (*Chenopodium album*), of which the leaves can be a substitute for spinach or cabbage, or can be dried for winter cattle fodder, and the seeds can be ground into flour using a *quern*. By this method grains were crushed between two stones to make flour, at first on flat or dished *saddle querns*, but from c.300BC using *beehive* or *rotary querns* which operated on a millstone principle *(fig.9)*.

Remarkable evidence of 1st millennium BC cultivation survives around some settlements, particularly in the Cheviots and includes areas where the ground appears to have been ploughed smooth, to create a *tilth* or prepared soil for planting, or formed into narrow cultivation ridges known as *cord rig*. The Borders contain some of the best examples of these *(Plate 3)*, notably on two sites at Hut Knowe (Hownam). Here it would seem that prominent rigs had been cultivated in the last season before the site was abandoned, while adjacent faint rigs from the previous season had been left fallow as part of a crop rotation. In upper Tweeddale the enclosed field systems related to stone built settlements at Dreva Craig (Stobo), and Glenrath Hope (Manor) may also have been worked in rotation, with stock used to graze and manure the land after harvest or during fallow intervals.

Aerial photographs show that an extensive series of ditched fields was associated with the Roman military base at *Trimontium*, where excavations suggest that the garrison made some provision for growing their own food during the 2nd century AD. Rather elongated ditched fields have been identified at Sprouston, where they are associated with a *Dark Age* settlement. Such linear plots may have formed the basis of medieval open fields which were divided into parallel rigs with furrows between.

Whether produced at subsistence level or as part of a surplus, unused food would need to be stored to prevent it going off or being eaten by animals. Elsewhere specialised buildings were used, and seed corn was sometimes buried in pits, but none of these have been found in the Borders. On a household basis grain could have been kept in small granaries with raised floors to keep the produce dry and away from small animals. Roman forts would have stored food in the same way, but on a much larger scale; large rectangular granaries with elevated floors have been found at *Trimontium* and Cappuck (Oxnam). Some *hillforts* may have been places where communal farm produce was collected together for the community and later re-distributed.

Clothing

The earliest human remains are found in Africa, where neither clothes nor shelters are essential to survival. However, as the global human population expanded into cooler regions warm coverings would have been essential, particularly during the very cold conditions of the glacial periods. In addition to their value as food, the animals caught by hunter-gatherers provided a wealth of raw materials, including pelts, hair, feathers and leather, bone, antler, horn, sinew and glue, to augment those available from bark, flax, grasses and other vegetable fibres. From this range the first clothes were made, using stone knives, scrapers for cleaning skins, awls for piercing leather, and needles for sewing together pieces of fur or leather with sinews. The effect need not have been crude, for magnificent buckskin outfits decorated with fringes and beads and set off by feather head-dresses were worn in recent years by the plains Indians of North America who used the same technology and range of materials.

The introduction of domesticated sheep and goats by early farmers provided the raw material for woollen clothes, and a fine collection of jet buttons from a burial at Harehope (Eddleston) (*Plate 14*), dated to about 2,250BC, may be the earliest indirect evidence for textiles from the Borders. Carding combs and spindle whorls were used to untangle wool and spin it into thread, and have been found on later sites, such as at *Trimontium*, where abundant leather shoes and pieces of armour show that the clothing of the Roman army had to meet special requirements.

Shelter

Mobile peoples need shelter, but their way of life required that this had to be collapsable and movable. No evidence has yet been found of this aspect of early life in the Borders, but we may imagine that wooden-framed tents of skin, bark or felt like the *tepees* of North America or the *yurts* of Mongolia could have been used, perhaps floored with furs or mats made of vegetable fibre.

Having no need to move at frequent intervals, farmers were able to build permanent homes near to their fields. Although rectangular structures are associated with the earliest stages of farming, the architecture which was to dominate the later prehistoric period in Britain was based upon circular buildings, and may have been developed from *tepee*-like skin tents of hunter-gatherers, although in the Borders no round house has been dated earlier than the 2nd millennium BC. Walled with clay daub and covered with thatch, these houses would have been warm and could be 15m (49ft) and more in diameter, with the conical roof as much as 10m (33ft) above the ground; although they probably lacked windows, a central hearth would have helped to brighten the gloomy interior.

With the Roman army came different building techniques, employing large structures capable of sheltering many men, rectangular building plans, and mortared stonework. Although the way of life of Anglian settlers was probably more like that of native Britons than Romans, the architecture of their buildings was also based on rectangles. Only a few examples of such buildings have so far been identified in the Borders and all of these come from two sites at Sprouston and Philiphaugh (Selkirk).

Transport

People were not confined to travel on foot or by canoe. Horses had been broken in before the end of the Ice Age, as is shown on a *palaeolithic* cave painting at La Marche in France, and a solid wooden wheel from Blair Drummond (Perthshire) shows that horse or ox drawn vehicles were in use by 1,000BC. Metal fittings from a miniature wagon with spoked wheels from Horsehope (Manor) date to the $8^{th}/7^{th}$ century BC, and metalwork found at several places in the Borders shows that fast two horse chariots were in use a few centuries later. The Roman army brought with them various vehicles, but none represent a significant improvement on those which were already in use by the native population.

No boats have been found in the Borders, although a paddle or oar was found at *Trimontium*. Finds from Yorkshire show that water transport had evolved beyond the skin boats of early hunters, and

Fig.10 *Polished stone axes like these from Cunzierton (Oxnam) helped early farmers to establish living space in the extensive forests. © The Trustees of the National Museums of Scotland 1997.*

sophisticated craft made of planks were in use in river estuaries on the east coast as early as the mid-2nd millennium BC. Such boats were propelled by paddles, and did not apparently have sails. When sails were first used in Britain is not known, but if the principle was not developed independently, it would surely have been learned from early visits by continental trading vessels, long before the sea-going craft of Roman, Irish and Germanic invaders arrived in the 1st millennium AD.

Tools

For day to day tasks a tool kit was available which saw marked improvement through time. The unique discovery in 1991, in the Alps, of a late stone age man preserved where he died of exposure about 5,000 years ago, revealed that he carried his shoes and clothing, a bow and quiver full of arrows, a back pannier, an early metal axe, fire lighting equipment, and the equivalent of a Swiss Army penknife: a stone knife in a wooden handle, a flint sharpener, a bone awl, and various blades and spare sinews. The more durable elements of such a kit are represented in the Borders by stone blades, axes, arrowheads and small *microliths*, which hunter-gatherers used to tip spears and arrows.

The advent of farming and an essentially sedentary lifestyle saw a progression to more effective polished stone tools, particularly axes *(fig.10),* and the adoption of pottery containers. Discoveries of polished axes show that the first farming communities spanned the full length and breadth of the region *(fig.14)*. Also distinctive of this period are the many leaf-shaped arrowheads which have been recovered from the Borders.

Wood, antler and bone artefacts were also widely used but due to their perishable nature, particularly in acid soils, are only likely to survive in waterlogged deposits which the archaeologist rarely has an opportunity to examine. A major exception is the wooden bow discovered in a peat hag at Rotten Bottom in the Tweedsmuir Hills in 1989. It was made of yew wood, had measured 1.78m in length,

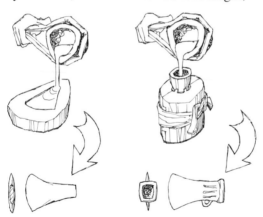

Fig.11 *Early metalworkers used flat open moulds, but in the 2ⁿᵈ millennium BC multiple-piece moulds enabled them to expand their range of products.*

and had been thrown away by its owner after it had broken during use. Wood from the bow has been *carbon dated* to between 3,140 and 2,940BC *(Plate 4)*.

Knowledge of metals, particularly copper with its tin alloy, bronze, and eventually iron, opened the way to the development of far more effective tools. The earliest bronze artefacts consisted of simple axes,

daggers and awls which were cast in flat moulds, but in time more complex castings and a greater range of tools was made possible by the use of composite moulds *(fig.11)*. By the early 1ˢᵗ millennium BC better castings and objects of bronze sheet could be produced by adding small amounts of lead to the molten metal, and three sheet bronze shields from Yetholm were made in this way.

Once knowledge of iron working had been introduced, probably during the 7ᵗʰ century BC, ores could be exploited much more widely than before, since iron ore even occurs as *pan* formations in bogs. Even so, metals were very precious during later prehistory, and worn out or broken objects would be re-cast or re-wrought, leaving very few on settlement sites for later archaeologists to find. An iron spearhead from Hayhope Knowe (Morebattle) is a notable exception.

The metal and wood working skills required to make new forms of artefact were developed by specialists, who had a wide range of equipment at their disposal. Use of the lathe for wood turning may have encouraged the production of wooden vessels at the expense of pottery development. Production of a complex piece, such as a chariot, would have required the skills of a carpenter, a bronze worker, a blacksmith, and a leather worker. By the time Roman soldiers arrived in the Borders the natives already had everyday tools and the skills to use them.

Society and Settlement

Archaeological evidence has its limitations, and our view of how early peoples were organised is based in part on observation of living communities at varying stages of development. *Bands, tribes, chiefdoms* and *states* show increasingly complex social structure with correspondingly larger populations *(fig.12)*.

Bands

Early hunter-gatherers were probably organised into "*bands*" of extended family groupings like those found today among Kalahari bushmen, or Australian aborigines.

Typically, such *bands* are made up of fewer than 100 individuals, due to their need for mobility in pursuit of food. In such small groups there is no great social distinction between individuals, leadership is informal and based on age and kinship, and members defer to the head of the family, whether female *(matriarch)* or male *(patriarch)*. Marriage within the group is avoided and partners are sought among other groups with neighbouring or overlapping hunting grounds, this being the occasion for special meetings between *bands*.

Tribes

Simple organisation in *bands* did not meet the needs of the larger population which developed after the adoption of farming around 4,000 BC. Instead of single extended families, this larger population contained groups of many families, which together formed a "*tribe*" numbering perhaps up to a few thousand individuals, distributed among small family-based farmsteads. Individual families would have been integrated into the wider society through marriage ties. Leaders were now selected on the basis of ability as well as age and kinship. That levels of society were beginning to emerge is suggested by the burial practices of these early communities, for although the massive *long cairns* of early farmers operated as communal tombs, they can only have served a minority of the population, and the majority must have been treated in a less grandiose manner. Examples of this type of social organisation can still be seen today among the New Guinea Highlanders and the Nuer and Dinka peoples of East Africa.

Chiefdoms

The relative simplicity of these earliest farming communities altered as the population increased, perhaps to many thousands, and developed into more complex *chiefdoms*. Individuals buried with special objects under a mound and massive ceremonial monuments *(henges)* built with the co-ordinated labour of many were characteristic of a multi-ranked society which emerged in the 3rd millennium BC. In such societies a governing chief (leaders are usually, but not exclusively, male) has greater power and is chosen for his ability and kinship with his predecessor. Social position is

Social Structures

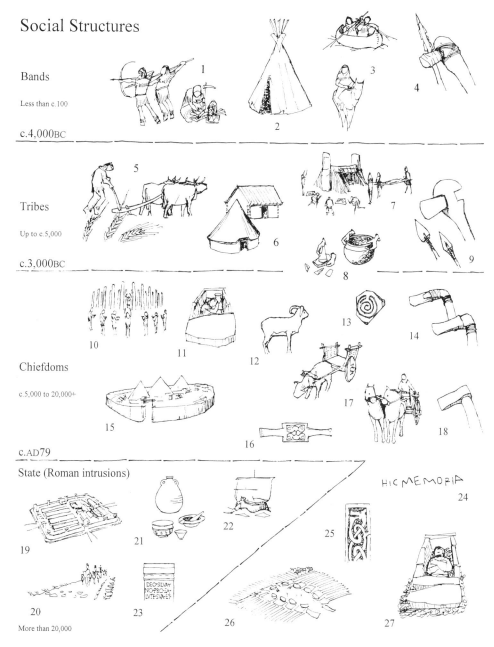

Bands

Less than c.100

c.4,000BC

Tribes

Up to c.5,000

c.3,000BC

Chiefdoms

c.5,000 to 20,000+

c.AD79

State (Roman intrusions)

More than 20,000

Fig.12 *Early societies developed as population increased, and material culture changed with time: (1) hunter-gatherers; (2) bark or hide tents and containers; (3) horse riding and canoes; (4) flaked stone tools; (5) cereal cultivation and domesticated animals; (6) permanent houses; (7) communal tombs; (8) pottery; (9) developed stone tools; (10) ceremonial monuments; (11) individual crouched burials from c.2,500BC; (12) woollen clothing; (13) decorated boulder, Ancrum, 3rd millennium BC; (14) bronze tools from c.2,500 BC; (15) enclosed settlements of round houses, 1st millennium BC; (16) enamelled horse brass, Eckford, c.1st century AD; (17) carts and chariots, 1st millennium BC; (18) iron tools from c.650 BC; (19) Roman military fort and (20) strategic road; (21) commercial pottery and (22) increased continental trade; (23) inscribed stone altar, Newstead, 2nd century AD; (24) inscribed tombstone, Yarrow, 5th century AD; (25) decorated stone cross, Jedburgh, 7th century AD; (26) nucleated Anglian village with rectangular buildings; (27) Christian extended burial.*

determined by relationship to the chief, so even the young can enjoy high status. Historical examples of this kind of society can be found among the Northwest Coast Indians in the USA or in the *chiefdoms* of 18th century Tonga, Tahiti and Hawaii.

The fighting prowess of individuals probably contributed to their overall status, and axes were early symbols of power, although many were to be displayed rather than used *(fig.10)*. Warfare can be a largely symbolic activity among simple societies, but the issues at stake between rival *chiefdoms* could have led to serious fighting, and there is no doubting the defensible possibilities of Borders *hillforts* in the 1st millennium BC.

Whether such sites were purely refuges from attack, or also operated as status symbols, store houses, or all three, they were the product of growing populations in which competition for prestige and power were influential factors. Land had great value, and boundaries between neighbouring settlements indicate a territorial awareness. The trouble taken to construct linear earthworks to augment natural landscape features, such as water courses, reflects the increasing importance placed upon territories by their owners in a climate of rising population. Perhaps the most striking expression of personal power are defended buildings, the stone *broch* towers and *duns*, of which a few are to be found in the Borders. They were not typical of the region, and represent ideas imported from further north and west, and as such may have reflected the personal aspirations of their owners.

The Roman State and After

At intervals from c.AD79 until the early 3rd century the region formed part of the Roman Empire, a sophisticated *state* society with a population of millions. From written accounts of the period we know that during their incorporation into the Roman province of Britannia the native people of this region were the (perhaps) unwilling subjects of a distant Emperor, subject to the legislation of a *state* bureaucracy and liable to taxation and tribute. Lasting features of this system were the road network constructed to enforce military conquest, and the sites of military bases, particularly at *Trimontium*, Lyne *(Plate 6)* and Oakwood (Selkirk). Frontier works are characteristic of such societies, and the Borders fell between the successive walls of Hadrian (ruled AD117-138) and Antoninus Pius (ruled AD138-161). In view of the exposed position of this, Rome's most northerly province, Roman civilians would have constituted a small minority in proportion to the large numbers of soldiers which were required to maintain Roman rule. Although for most of the period of Roman Britain the frontier lay to the south of Hadrian's Wall, many coins and metal objects have been found in the Borders which indicate that some form of commercial contact may have continued between the two areas.

The native population of the Borders seems to have lacked any enthusiasm for the civilian trappings of the Roman *state*, such as towns and country villas, and this suggests that the older *chiefdom* structure re-emerged when the Romans withdrew. This situation may not have been radically altered when Anglian supremacy was established in the 6th and 7th centuries AD, as the kingdom of *Bernicia* was still essentially a sophisticated *chiefdom*. The site at Sprouston (*figs.32 & 33)* may have played a central role in administration at a local level, and resembles the site of King Edwin's palace at Yeavering (Northumberland).

By political and military processes *Bernicia* and its neighbouring kingdoms were gradually fused into the two separate kingdoms of Scotland and England. The "learning" which was a feature of the Christian church in *Bernicia*, after the conversion of King Edwin in AD626, not only led to the writings of the Venerable Bede and others, distinguishing this as an historic, as distinct from prehistoric, society, but also provided one of the central tools from which to develop from a *chiefdom* society to a *state*.

Settlement patterns

The remains which people of different periods have left behind can be more easily understood when their numbers, their social organisation, and their needs are clear.

The milder climates of valleys, their deeper and more fertile soils, and the importance of rivers, primarily as a source of water and food, but also as a channel of communication, attracted settlers from the first (*figs.13, 14, 16, 17*).

Hunters and Pioneers

Stone tools and flakes of hunter-gatherers have been collected from ploughed field surfaces, particularly those close to rivers and lochs, although such finds may also await discovery in areas of upland where the soil is seldom exposed (*fig.13)*. These sites probably include seasonally occupied base camps, and smaller, specialised sites for such activities as dealing with animal carcasses or making tools and other equipment. An example of the latter might be Flint Hill (Stobo), where *chert* was exploited in the prehistoric period.

It is interesting that no coastal sites have yet been discovered in Borders, even though these would be a source of food throughout the year, and many are known on the west coast.

The Borders could have accommodated different *bands* which shared the same, or overlapping hunting grounds, and harboured no proprietorial feelings over the land. At the Rink (Galashiels) a particularly large spread of tools and flakes suggests that the junction of the Ettrick with the Tweed was a favoured place, and may have been where different *bands* used to meet on special occasions. A similar site may have existed at the junction of the Tweed with the Teviot.

Hunter-gatherer sites in the Borders c.8000BC - c.4000BC

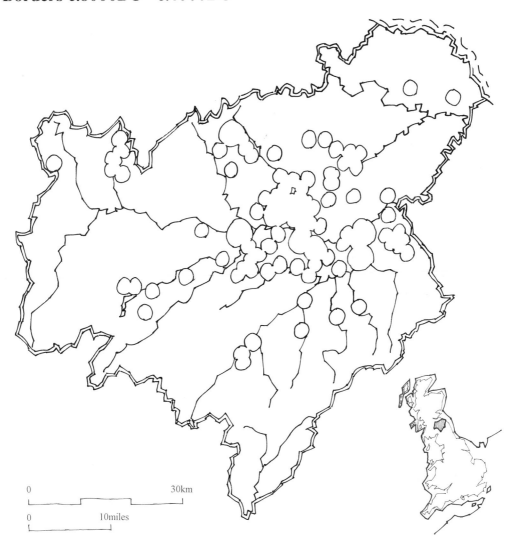

Fig 13   *Hunter-gatherer bands reached the Borders when Britain was still joined to the continent, and evidence of their camps comes mostly from river sides. Sites with many artefacts (represented by larger symbols) may have been base camps or meeting places.*

Early Farmers in the Borders
c.4000BC - 2000BC

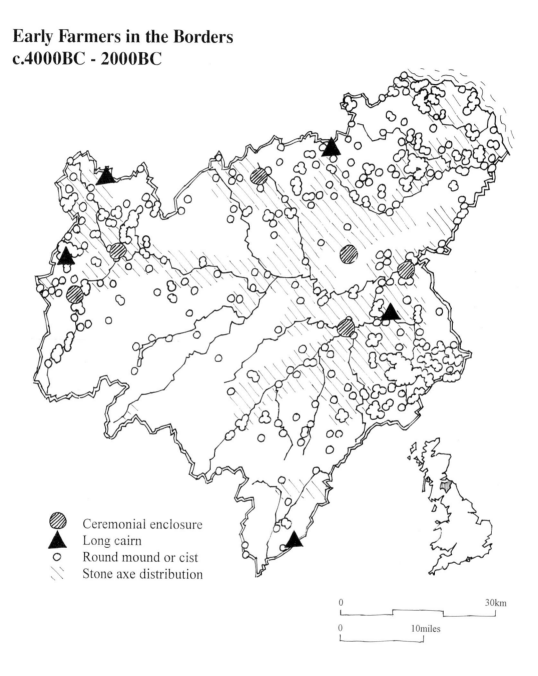

Ceremonial enclosure
Long cairn
Round mound or cist
Stone axe distribution

0   30km

0   10miles

Fig.14   *Stone axe distribution, although limited to modern arable land, indicates that valleys were settled by early farmers, whose communal long cairns and individual burials were often sited on hills. Three concentrations of burial and ceremonial sites in the Lammermuir Hills, upper Tweeddale, and the Teviotdale/eastern Cheviots area suggest territories of emerging chiefdoms .*

Sense of territory may not have evolved before the creation of permanent settlements by developing *tribes* of early farmers. Evidence of their impact on the woodland is provided by finds, from modern arable fields, of polished stone axes (superior to the chipped axes of hunter-gatherers), although this distribution would have extended into areas which are now covered by pasture or modern forestry.

The few *long cairns* which are known in the Borders can scarcely have been burial places for the whole social group, although they may have operated as *tribal* ceremonial centres. Significantly, single burials and ceremonial enclosures, which are a characteristic development within *chiefdom* societies, show some concentration close to, or in the general neighbourhood of *long cairns (fig.14)*. Distinctive clusters in the upper Tweed, in the Lammermuir Hills, and in the Teviotdale-Cheviot foothills area might be taken as an indication of where the bulk of the population was concentrated by c.2,000BC.

Filling up the landscape

Most of the visible settlement remains in the Borders are located in upland grazing, where differences may be chronological or due to local variation. A type of settlement found in Peeblesshire consists of circular houses terraced into the hillside, and at Green Knowe (Eddleston) a settlement of this form has been *radiocarbon* dated to c.1,500BC. In the Cheviot Hills different types of settlement occur, where the variation is explained by their date.

The uplands can support settlement, but more exposed positions, precarious farming conditions, and remoteness from more fertile valley locations and social networks make the prospect unattractive. Abandoned settlements show that there were various periods when attempts were made to live in these marginal areas, with areas of *cord rig* and *cultivation terraces* bearing witness that these settlements were not wholly dependent upon livestock.

In the earlier 1st millennium BC round houses, sometimes enclosed by palisades, are found adjacent to *cord rig* cultivation *(Plate 3)*. After about 500BC stone walled forts or embanked enclosures were constructed, sometimes on the site of an earlier palisaded enclosure, as at Hownam Rings (Hownam) and Hayhope Knowe. In both periods the enclosure of settlements suggests that security was an important reason for moving out of the valley, and growing numbers of people may have been in fierce competition for the available land. If so, this seems to have been resolved, perhaps with the establishment of stronger central control, for the last phase of prehistoric settlement on the Cheviots consists mostly of undefended clusters of round houses and adjoining yards. In a number of places disputes over territory had been resolved by the construction of linear earthworks where clear natural demarcation features, such as burns, were absent.

Fig.15 *Typical of the ancient landscapes which survive from the 1ˢᵗ millennium BC in the Cheviot Hills are neighbouring hillforts at Camp Tops and Hayhope Knowe with adjacent cord rig and sunken roads, and cultivation terraces and an undefended settlement on the lower slopes.*

Although located on hills, the distribution of forts reflects the river network, rather than the watersheds in between, and there are large numbers in the central Borders *(figs.15 & 16)*. These appear to be separated from upper Tweeddale and the eastern Lammermuir Hills by thinly populated areas which suggest "buffer zones". Similar low levels of population are implied in Ettrick, Yarrow and the head of Liddesdale.

These three concentrations imply separate populations or political entities, and those on the east and west are actually larger in area, because the sites which they represent extend beyond the boundaries of the Borders.

The locations chosen by the Roman army for their forts, and the lines taken for their strategic roads effectively neutralised any threat that these peoples might combine and threaten the conquerors *(fig.16)*. The western and central groups were pinned down by strategic roads (broadly on the lines of the modern A702 and A68) and by garrisons, which effectively outflanked those people living in the eastern Lammermuir Hills, where they were also vulnerable to attack from the sea.

Native Britons and the Roman Army
1st to 3rd centuries AD.

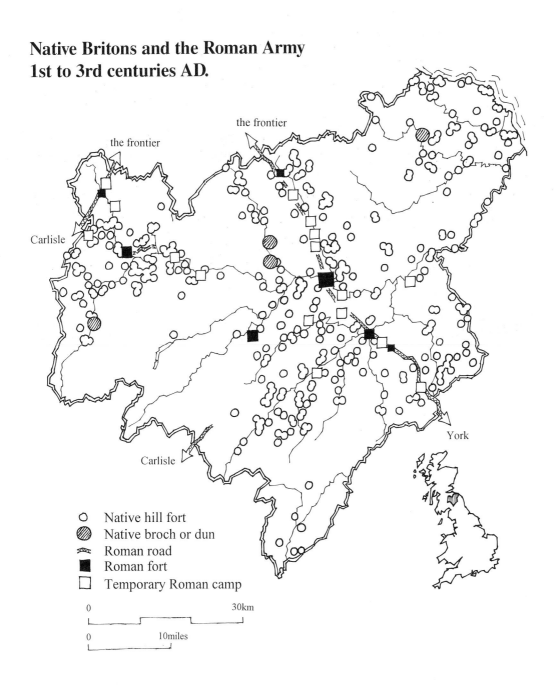

Fig.16 *Hillfort distribution suggests that by the time of the first Roman invasion the central Borders may have been a political entity in itself, with other groups occupying the eastern Lammermuir Hills and upper Tweeddale. Roman conquest established a firm hold on the central and western areas with strategic roads and fortified garrisons, but left the eastern block alone.*

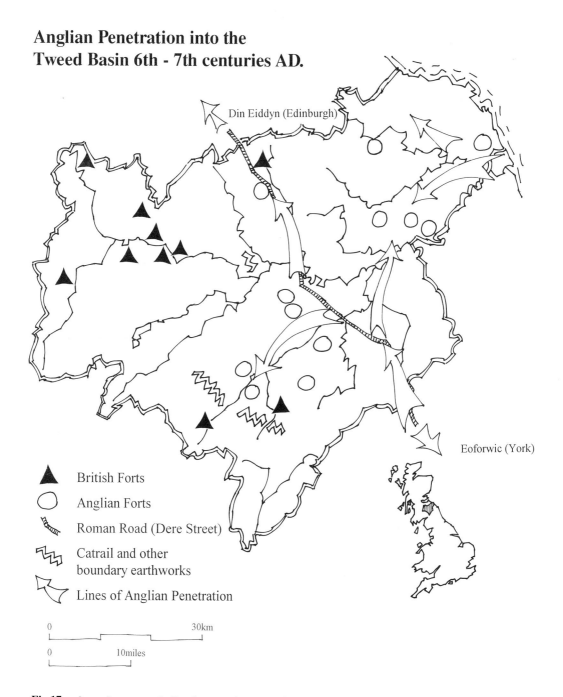

Anglian Penetration into the Tweed Basin 6th - 7th centuries AD.

Din Eiddyn (Edinburgh)

Eoforwic (York)

▲ British Forts

○ Anglian Forts

Roman Road (Dere Street)

Catrail and other boundary earthworks

Lines of Anglian Penetration

0   30km

0   10miles

Fig.17   *In post-Roman centuries Dere Street was the main north-south road, along which Anglian settlers arrived in the Borders. Their forts (caestrs) can still be distinguished from their British counterparts (caers) by name, and suggest the territories occupied by natives and incomers, who may have been divided by frontier earthworks such as the Catrail.*

During the Roman occupations the native population was administered from Roman military posts, although there are signs that some sort of civilian settlement may have existed at *Trimontium*.

Anglian settlements are barely known from archaeological remains, although place names indicate where settlements may be concealed beneath historic villages. This is particularly the case with villages such as Hownam, Edrom and Midlem, which once contained the Anglian word *ham*. Other place names from the 6th or 7th century AD are those which derive from *ceastr* (fort) *(fig.17)*, although they do not confirm that fortifications were still occupied when they were named.

Ideology and Beliefs

Religious ceremonial and burial practices were closely linked in antiquity, as indeed they are today. Ritual monuments tended to attract burials in the same way that Christian churches stand amid, and around graves. Unlike Christianity, which is well documented, most ancient pagan rituals and the beliefs which were associated with them have been lost, unless they survive, unrecognised in folk tradition. Most of our knowledge of prehistoric religion is based upon archaeological records of structures and objects.

Hunting and Fertility

Hunter-gatherer bands have left no recognisable ceremonial monuments in Britain, and finds of human bone are rare.

The most celebrated formal burial of these people was found in a cave in South Wales which has been *carbon dated* to around 20,000 years ago, and evidence from Star Carr in Yorkshire from the 9th millennium BC includes a deer antler mask which could have formed part of a ceremonial costume. These finds suggest that the religious beliefs of hunter-gatherers may have paid particular attention to the chase. This would be consistent with cave paintings in France and elsewhere which show animals and hunting scenes and were painted between 30,000BC and 10,000BC.

Ancestors and Astronomy

Hunter-gatherers may have exposed the bodies of their dead on raised platforms, similar to the custom of some Plains Indians of North America, but there is evidence that early farmers, who built the oldest of our surviving funeral monuments, also followed this tradition. Their stone *long cairns*, such as the Mutiny Stones (Longformacus) *(Plate 7)*, and earthen *long barrows* were constructed in the 4th millennium BC to contain the collected bones from such exposed (*excarnated*) bodies. These cairns were by no means common - only five have been recognised in the Borders *(fig.14)* - and some may not have contained burials. Like Christian churches, such monuments may have also served as a focus for religious ceremonial, and their final form probably conceals a complex history of development.

Although burial in these communal tombs would have been a privilege not afforded to the whole population, individual status was not marked by special grave goods, and the tradition may have embodied a strong element of ancestor worship. Some of these tombs were designed to line up with the rising or setting of the sun or moon at special times, and this interest in astronomy was probably related to the agricultural calendar and the fertility of land.

Ceremonial complexes, linked to a tradition of individual crouched burials accompanied by special objects, reflect the emergence of *chiefdom* societies. Massive monuments, sometimes with astronomical significance, were constructed in extensive clearings. At Meldon Bridge (Lyne) the confluence of the River Tweed and Lyne Water formed a focus for standing stones, a massive palisade which defined a promontory of 8ha (20acres), and burial monuments. Elsewhere circular earthworks, or *henges* **(Plate 8)** were structures which needed the co-ordinated efforts of many people over a long period. A *henge* found by aerial photography at Mellerstain (Earlston) is a similar focus for other enclosures, and forms part of an alignment with standing stones on Brotherstone Hill (Mertoun/Smailholm).

As this phase progressed the popularity of individual burial grew, and later graves contained decorated pottery *food vessels* and *beakers* as well as the earliest metal objects from the region. Such graves were usually covered by mounds, often on prominent positions such as White Meldon (Eddleston), Dirrington Great Law (Longformacus) or Eildon Mid Hill (Bowden), but a cemetery of seven stone *cists* from West Water Reservoir (West Linton) was marked by a boulder rather than a cairn. In most of these the body had been crouched, as though asleep, but some graves contained cremated bodies, perhaps because they died some way from the traditional burial place, or at the wrong season. Pollen grains found with burials show that flowers were also put into some graves.

Weather and Water

The construction of large ceremonial monuments and the practice of individual burial in flat cemeteries or under mounds came to an end in about 1,500BC. How the dead were treated thereafter is obscure, but objects which might once have formed grave goods, such as metal weapons, have been found as ritual offerings in rivers, springs and pools. This may have been due to the onset of wetter climatic conditions which recreated marshes and pools that had dried up during the earlier period. Examples of such offerings from the Borders include three bronze shields from Yetholm and a decorated bronze collar from Stichill all of which were discovered in boggy ground which had formerly been open water.

These traditions lasted throughout the rest of the prehistoric period, and recent excavations at Newstead have shown that outside the Roman fort of *Trimontium* offerings of complete objects and animal skulls were made before old wells were filled in *(Plate 10)*. This may have been to placate fertility gods which the Romans revered, although it may represent a conscious respect for the Eildon Hills and the springs around their base, where several Christian holy wells now exist *(fig.28)*.

Although no *bog bodies* have been recognised in the Borders, a skull from peaty ground near Lauder, and records of weapons and bones from a moss near Lilliesleaf could be evidence that not only objects but also human beings were offered to the water spirits. Wet places were also mysterious to the Angles of *Northumbria* as is evident from surviving literature, such as *Beowolf*, in which *Grendel's* pool plays an important part. The earlier British tradition of offering weapons to water spirits is most familiar in the story of *Arthur*, whose sword Excalibur was received by the spirit of the waters at his death. We still preserve the tradition today, although with more modest offerings to wishing wells.

Although hunting, ancestors, astronomy and water seem to have been the main themes of religious beliefs at different times, it is likely that some prominent landscape features also had special significance, perhaps from the earliest times when they afforded rare views across the forested wilderness. As trees were cleared particular interest may have been taken in such hills as the Eildons and

Rubers Law (Hawick/Cavers) because of their distinctive shapes *(Plate 2)*. Both sites have springs and holy wells around them, have produced hoards of metalwork, and have evidence of Roman structures which are usually interpreted as signal stations or watch towers, but could have been shrines. Other Roman masonry, usually interpreted as evidence of a temple or monument, has been found at Langlee (Galashiels), and a stone figure, possibly of the god Mars, was found at Minto.

In the later Roman period Christianity became the official religion of the Empire, and it continued to have a foothold after the British provinces became independent. Christian tradition orientates burials west-east, and a series of graves with long *cists* in this alignment was found in Yarrow, not far from an inscribed stone recording the burials of Nudus and Dumnogenus, the princely sons of Liberalis. This inscription, and others from Liddesdale and the valley of the Manor Water are relics of post-Roman Christianity, when the ministry of St Ninian made an impact upon the inhabitants of 5th century Britain.

Even early Christians preferred to use traditional religious sites, and Yarrow is also the site of two standing stones from an earlier period. At Sprouston a prehistoric ceremonial complex was chosen as the site of an apparently Christian settlement, and could owe much to the ministry of St Paulinus, who preached Christianity throughout the kingdom of *Northumbria* in the 7th century

AD, and heralded a period exceptional for its churches and its art.

The Christianity of the *Early Historic* period is described by contemporary writers, such as Bede, but without such written records, archaeology can never give us the names of the deities worshipped by ancient societies, nor the details of their mythology. It does, however, illustrate pervasive and powerful religious beliefs throughout human history, and the repeated recourse to supernatural agencies, to protect against disease, natural disaster and fear of the unknown.

Oral Traditions and Art

Although not necessarily written down, most cultures have myths and legends that are passed on by word of mouth from generation to generation. Even today wisdom is passed on as "old wives' tales" and apocryphal stories circulate as "urban legends". The antiquity and history of language itself is far from clear, and place names of British, English, Irish and Scandinavian derivation show how mixed are the cultural origins of the Borders.

The ability of trained poets and bards to memorise whole sagas and epic poems preserved many ancient traditions until they could be set down in writing, usually by Christian monks. Such legendary figures as *Chu Chulainn*, *Arthur*, *Merlin* and *Beowolf* have come to us from different traditions in this way.

Strong oral traditions have left the Borders with a wealth of tales from the middle ages and later, but although we may lack stories from earlier times, word of mouth has left many place names. Rivers such as the Ale, Allan, White- and Black- Adder, and perhaps Tweed and Ettrick are the earliest names which survive in the region. Like the Mississippi and Potomac in America, these names could have been used by hunter-gatherers and adopted by later linguistic groups. It is only known that some of them have similar linguistic origins to continental rivers and are older than the early form of modern Welsh, generally referred to as *Cumbric*, which was the native tongue when Roman soldiers first arrived in the area. Place names which include such elements as *caer*: 'fort', *tref*: 'homestead, village', or *pen*: 'hill' (e.g. Cardrona, Traquair, (both Traquair), Penchrise (Cavers)) belong to this *Cumbric* tongue, which was in turn eclipsed by English as the language of the Borders. Some Old English place names incorporate the words *caester*: 'fort' and *ham*: 'homestead' (e.g. Bonchester (Hobkirk) and Midlem (Bowden)), and originated during the *Northumbrian* period.

Visual arts were also important to the early settlers and, in addition to their obvious aesthetic value, a great deal of information and symbolism was imbedded in their work. Prehistoric art from the Borders survives on carved stones, decorated pottery and a range of metalwork and other artefacts, and fragmentary survivals from other areas show that woodwork and textiles were also subject to artistic treatment.

Fig.18 *This rare example of rock art was found at Ancrum and dates from the third millennium* BC. *It was not merely decorative, but probably formed an important symbolic element of a funerary or ceremonial monument.*

Early rock art in the Borders is not abundant and is confined to stones which have been detached from the bedrock. The small range of motifs employed includes cup-shaped hollows, rings, cups and rings in combination, and spirals. They occur on boulders or on flat slabs, and examples from Drumelzier and Peebles were built into burial *cists*. The most recent find, a spiral on a boulder from Ancrum *(fig.18)* is now in Wilton Lodge Museum, (Hawick).

These simple geometric forms also occur in Northumberland and Argyll where they are pecked into the living rock, and there is little doubt that the symbols were highly significant to early farmers. Similar symbols were used to decorate *grooved ware* pottery in the 3rd millennium BC, and this pottery is a characteristic find from ceremonial sites. Other early decorated pottery forms include *beakers, food vessels* and *cinerary urns*, *(Plate 11)* all of which types are believed to have enjoyed high status, frequently associated with burial, before being more widely available for domestic use. Such burials also include occasional jewellery, such as the necklace of *cannel coal* and lead beads from West Water Reservoir or the necklace composed of jet beads and spacer plates from Priest's Crown (Eckford).

Development of bronze working created opportunities for ornament, but this is very restrained and broadly limited to socketed axes ornamented with pendants, and shields textured with small dome-shaped knobs in concentric rings. After c.400BC however, British *La Tène* art developed into a rich and distinctive series of flowing curvilinear styles, often called "Celtic". Particularly fine is part of a gold neck ring (*torc*) from Netherurd (Kirkurd) and a bronze collar from Stichill *(Plate 9)*. During this period enamel was used to decorate armlets, brooches and horse harness, and glass was used for beads and bracelets.

Roman technology extended the range of native products, particularly in the use of glass and enamelled bronzes, but there is no evidence that it led to any revival of stone-carving skills. Classical Roman inscriptions appear on altars and other commemorative stones from military sites, but the outstanding piece of sculpture is a carved marble head found at Hawkshaw (Tweedsmuir), which may be loot brought north from a raid into the Roman province.

Post-Roman sculpture is Christian-influenced and includes the crudely carved *Orans* (praying) figure from Over Kirkhope (Yarrow), which belongs to the 5th-6th century AD, and various Anglian cross fragments decorated with *interlace* ornament or *zoomorphic* dragon shapes which are the product of the establishment of the church within the kingdom of *Northumbria*.

Outside Contacts

Although much of the Borders is isolated hill country, penetrated by the tributaries of the Tweed and Liddel, but shielded by ridges from its nearest neighbours, at no time has the population of the area lived in total isolation. However organised, the population has enjoyed links with neighbouring groups, and these assisted not only the spread of new ideas concerning technology and ideology, but also the exchange of commodities. The clearest archaeological evidence for these links consists of raw materials, some of which show very early that the exchange of goods and ideas.

The first settlers into the region moved along natural corridors formed by river valleys which developed into "trade" routes in and out of the area. Hunter-gatherers used pitchstone from the west of Scotland on sites in Peeblesshire, Roxburghshire and Lauderdale. This way of life changed when, *via* routes from the continent, the first farming communities began to form, growing cereals and raising new breeds of animals, and using stone axes from the English Lake District and other sources to clear the forests. Examples of these axes have been found at Borthwick Hall (Heriot) and Old Caverton (Eckford).

Hunting bands and early farmers probably exchanged goods when they met, but as hierarchical societies developed contact was more likely to be through the leaders who redistributed goods among their followers. By this means highly placed members of society obtained prestige items which strengthened their social positions. Such items include jadeite axes (from Brittany or the Rhineland) which were found at Greenlawdean and Cunzierton (Oxnam) *(fig.10)* and an arrowhead of Antrim porcellanite from the Young Plantation (Selkirk). Gold, amber, jet, *faience* and other valuable materials have been found in graves of the early 2nd millennium BC. By 500BC the range of prestige goods probably included coral and glass from the Mediterranean area. Other commodities may have included salt from coastal areas. What goods were being traded in exchange is not known, but they could have included slaves.

The approach of the Roman Empire introduced professional trading through a market, in which coinage augmented barter, and pottery, jewellery, glassware, ornate metalwork and other goods were mass-produced within Britain. In addition, a wide range of exotic imports reached the area from other parts of the Empire. Although the ease with which such communication was possible ceased with the Roman withdrawal from Britain, contacts were maintained through the Christian Church, and incorporation of part of the area into the Kingdom of *Northumbria* extended contacts once more into parts of southern Britain along the Roman road *Dere Street*.

Early Settlers in the Borders

Part 3:

Human Impact upon the Landscape

Although the shape of the Borders is provided by geological deposits, which are for the most part unseen, living plants not only provide most of the colour of the landscape, but also support, directly or indirectly, life itself. For humans plants not only provide food, but also the materials necessary to build shelters as well as many of the trappings of everyday life. Thus, from the earliest times people have made an impact upon the plants which make up so much of our environment.

Reconstructing the Ancient Environment

Although dead plants decay naturally with the assistance of fungi, bacteria and other organisms, if a plant dies and becomes buried in water-logged or otherwise airless conditions normal processes of decay slow down and often virtually stop. If it is left undisturbed it settles to the bottom, where, subjected to the pressure of further build up of plant material and silt, it eventually becomes peat *(fig.19)*. In peat bogs plant remains can survive for thousands of years in near-perfect condition and it is these remains, especially microscopic pollen grains, which scientists use to reconstruct the ancient landscape.

Pollen grains have distinctive shapes and a *palynologist* can often identify different types of trees, shrubs, grasses and herbs from the grains contained in a single sample from a peat bog *(fig.20)*. Peat forms

Fig.19 *Blanket peat on Borders Hills formed over thousands of years, and at Rotten Bottom, Tweedsmuir preserved pollen has revealed that hunter-gatherers roamed scrub-covered plateaux in search of game.*

Pollen and Ancient Environments

Pollen proportions in a peat bog

Pollen grains
(at a magnification of 1,000 times).

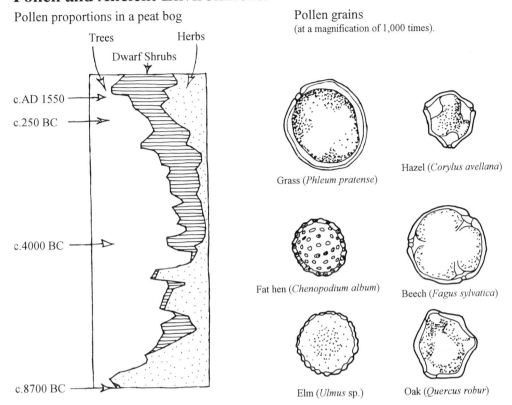

Fig.20 *Distinctive pollen grains (right) found in cores taken from peat bogs indicate the proportions in which different local plant species lived. The oldest pollen come from the base of the core, and intervals in the development of the peat are dated by radiocarbon. Presented in diagramatic form (left), the changing ratio of tree, shrub and herb pollen from bottom to top equates with the growth of forest after the Ice Age, and its gradual clearance and replacement with shrubs and herbs. (After R Tipping and P Reynolds).*

over a very long time and the oldest plants are buried at the bottom, so samples from different levels within the peat will provide pollen in proportions which reflect the state of the vegetation at different times and in varying conditions.

All plants and animals absorb a radioactive isotope, Carbon-14, from the atmosphere, and when they die this begins to break down, decaying at a rate of 50% every 5,730 years (the *half life*). By measuring the Carbon-14 remaining in ancient

organic matter, such as wood, leather, or even bone, it is possible to provide an approximate date for the death of the plant, animal or person from which it came. Although a great many artefacts and other remains can be dated in this way, the method is particularly useful for dating the various levels of peat bogs, in which suitable material invariably occurs.

Other scientific methods are employed by archaeologists, and the most accurate also relies on the preservation of woody plant remains. Annual rings form on a tree every growing season and their thickness is governed by the temperature, rainfall and other factors, all of which vary from year to year. The pattern of rings in two trees of the same species, age and date from the same place will be identical, and will overlap with those of older and younger trees for those years when they were growing at the same time. This characteristic forms the basis of tree-ring dating (*dendrochronology*), by which the actual year when a tree was felled can sometimes be identified.

Scientific sampling, dating, and identification of plants from a single site is an expensive and time-consuming process, and is restricted by the availability of suitable sample areas. The Scottish Borders, however, have been the subject of considerable research and are now one of the best known areas in Scotland. These studies have revealed some details of how the environment has changed with the passing of time and provide a background with which to compare the archaeological evidence for human activity.

A general rise in temperature which began about 15,000 years ago brought about the end of the last period of glaciation. The ice may have disappeared from most of Britain and northern Europe in as little as a century, but temperatures fluctuated until they reached present day levels. The devastated landscape left by the ice underwent gradual changes as plants re-established themselves and new species appeared as the climate improved.

Something like this process can be seen in the changing temperature zones which exist on the slopes of a mountain. The ground above the tree line, covered with mosses, lichens and low-growing plants such as cloudberry (*Rubus chamaemorus*) and heather (*Calluna* sp.), resembling the *tundra* of the Arctic Circle of the present day, is the kind of environment which would have covered much of the Borders in the period immediately following the final retreat of the ice. Lower down the mountain slopes grasses, stunted shrubs, occasional willows (*Salix fragilis*) and birch (*Betula* sp.) precede mixed woodlands consisting of pine (*Pinus* sp.), birch, hazel (*Corylus avellana*), rowan (*Sorbus aucuparia*) and juniper (*Juniperus communis*), much like the vast forests of present day Canada and Scandinavia, and such was the vegetation cover when the first hunter-gatherers peopled the area about 10,000 years ago. Pine and birch cannot compete with oak (*Quercus* sp.), ash (*Fraxinus excelsior*) and holly (*Ilex aquifolium*) as the temperature improves, so they disappear at lower altitudes; lower still a rich woodland canopy exists, dominated by such tree species as oak, ash, wych elm (*Ulmus glabra*), wild cherry (*Prunus avium*) and blackthorn (*Prunus spinosa*), with alder (*Alnus glutinosa*) and willow growing in particularly wet locations. Such woodlands formed the natural cover of the British Isles by

Plate 1. The cliffs at St Abb's Head consist of volcanic rocks of the *Devonian* era, and are home to thousands of sea birds.

Plate 2. The curious isolation of some Borders hills, such as Black Hill (left) and the Eildons, is the result of their volcanic origin, and may have given rise to their veneration by early settlers.

Plate 3. The circular slot left by a wooden palisade represents a 2,500 year old settlement on the Cheviot Hills, and the corduroy texture of the vegetation around is caused by *cord rig* cultivation strips.

Plate 4. In 1991 Dan Jones of Melrose showed his find of a broken wooden hunting bow to archaeologists working near Galashiels. The bow, which he had found high in the Tweedsmuir Hills at Rotten Bottom (see ***Fig.19***), was later dated by *radiocarbon* to 4,000BC.

Plate 5. The large *hillfort* on Eildon Hill North contains nearly 300 hut platforms, which are clearly revealed under a covering of snow.

Plate 6. The Roman fort at Lyne was constructed in the early 2nd century AD, and the ramparts, although partly ploughed, still show a typical "playing card" plan.

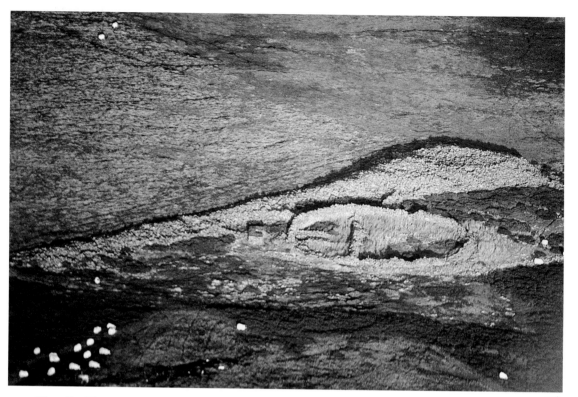

Plate 7. The Mutiny Stones, comprise a *long cairn*, or communal tomb, which was built by early farmers about 5,000 years ago. The 19th century sheep stell has been built of stone quarried from the cairn.

Plate 8. In this ploughed field at Channelkirk, soil marks reveal the existence of a levelled circular *henge*, a form of ceremonial monument which consisted of a circular ditched enclosure with the upcast bank on the outer side. Such monuments were important meeting places for early farmers.

Plate 9.   This magnificent bronze collar would have been made by a master craftsman at the end of the 1ˢᵗ millennium BC, and was placed in a bog at Stichill as a ritual offering.
© The Trustees of the National Museums of Scotland 1997.

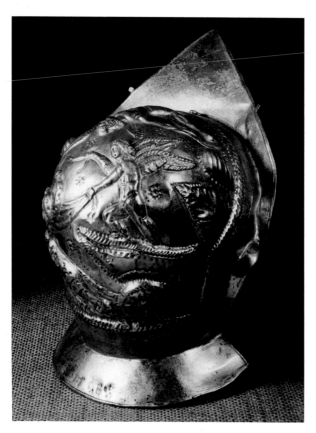

Plate 10.   This parade helmet was used by a Roman cavalryman at *Trimontium* for special ceremonies. It was one of a wide range of valuable objects placed in old wells, probably as good will offerings to deities to ensure future water purity.
© The Trustees of the National Museums of Scotland 1997.

Plate 11. Pottery was first made by early farming communities, and provided a medium for artistic decoration. These *food vessels* were made in the early 2nd millennium BC for inclusion in graves at West Linton. © The Trustees of the National Museums of Scotland 1997.

Plate 12. This defended farmstead at Whitrighill was favourably located to take advantage of a wide range of natural resources, which included fertile soils and an adjacent loch. The farm contained an impressive circular house which had thick stone walls and was paved with large blocks of basalt from nearby crags.

Plate 13. The Roman strategic road, *Dere Street* linked the military base at *Eburacum* (York) to the northern frontier. It still survives on Whitton Edge where ditches mark the sides and lines of pits beyond were quarried for road stone.

Plate 14. These jet buttons from Meldon valley were found in the grave of an early farmer, dated to c.2,250BC, and are all that survive of his clothes. The fine quality of the buttons reflects the importance of the deceased. ©The Trustees of the National Museums of Scotland 1997.

Plate 15. At Edin's Hall a *hillfort* is overlain by a later settlement in which embanked courts associated with round houses are dominated by the immense structure of a circular *broch* tower. © Crown copyright by courtesy of Historic Scotland.

Plate 16. Successive temporary camps, one inside the other, were constructed for Roman troops on the march beside *Dere Street* at Pennymuir. Each camp was enclosed by a bank and ditch with several entrances covered by traverses, or *tutuli*.

5,000BC, and would have remained so, but for the long and relentless encroachment of farming.

In their damp, dim interiors these developing woodlands provided shelter from strong winds and frost for many species of plants and animals. Even fallen or damaged trees provided a rich source of food for fungi and other dependent wild life. More light was able to break through the canopy around the woodland margins and in temporary clearings created by dying trees, and this enabled many more different varieties of shrubs and herbs to establish themselves. These opportunities reached their greatest extent when farming settlements had made extensive inroads, but before woodland became chronically depleted.

Woodland Clearance

It is difficult to imagine today that the landscape was once filled with trees, and that humans are largely responsible for their disappearance. No fragment of original forest survives, and even sites of "ancient woodland", such as Pease Dean (Cockburnspath), are of those places where the soil, plants and insects are distinctive of woodland and show that even though trees have been felled or have died, there has never been complete clearance. The oldest surviving Borders trees are found in Jed Forest, but these are only a few hundred years old. Most ancient woodland sites have survived only where the ground has been unsuitable for cultivation, particularly on steep valley sides and in other inaccessible places.

Hunter-gatherer *bands* drifted into the area in search of animals, and so gradual was the process of afforestation that the earliest may have followed game into the *tundra* from forest margins before woodland spread into the Borders area. Animals and small numbers of hunters would have had a limited impact on the tree cover, but their tracks and clearing could have become permanent. Natural breaks in the trees (by wind blow or forest fires), or deliberate clearings cut into established forest would have attracted animals to the better grazing offered by grasses and fruiting plants. This may have been particularly effective where thinner scree soils and sands with light shrub and tree cover enabled easier clearance by felling and grazing, and game drawn to such places in this way probably encouraged the creation of further clearings as a lure. The presence of such temporary clearings may be indicated by fluctuations in the amount of tree pollen at the Dod (Teviothead) about 8,000 years ago.

Although plant evidence consistently shows a reduction in tree pollen and an increase in grasses and herbs, the impact of farming is not nearly so clear cut as was once believed. A dramatic fall in the level of elm in about 4,000BC was once interpreted as the start of the *neolithic* period, and interpreted as an effect of intensive use of elm as animal food. It now appears more likely that the decline is due to a blight similar to Dutch Elm Disease, which has so devastated the species over the last thirty years.

Fig. 21 *The houses of early farmers could be elaborately furnished. Stone was used instead of timber at Skara Brae, Orkney, but box beds and dressers were modelled on perishable wooden types which would normally have been found in the Borders and other areas with abundant trees. (Photo: John Dent).*

The introduction of grazing animals during the 4th millennium BC had important implications for the recovery of trees where clearance had taken place, for unless precautions are taken to exclude sheep and other grazing or browsing animals they will eat the shoots of young trees and kill them. The failure of secondary woodland to reclaim many clearings led to the establishment of permanent open grazing, represented in the fossil pollen record by grasses and herbs. Any decline in the fertility of cultivated areas would, in the longer term, have led to further encroachment on the woodland. The extent of clearance may also have led to changes in building methods.

Wood is much easier than stone to obtain and work, and stone buildings are still rare in countries with abundant forests, such as parts of North America and Scandinavia. When trees are abundant, so is timber, which needs decades to grow. Early settlers would have used timber whenever it was available, and would have had no need to do more than trim tree trunks and use them to build log cabins (a building type which, incidentally, need leave little or no archaeological trace). Although early farmers at Skara Brae in Orkney made use of easily split coastal rocks to build their houses, this was because of the scarcity of trees on the islands, not necessarily because they preferred to use stone. Even so, the layout of furniture within the living rooms shows that such houses were modelled on wooden forms that may have been common in the Borders and elsewhere in Scotland *(fig.21)*.

Wherever trees grew such early domestic architecture would have been based upon the ready availability of timber. Houses were built with wooden walls and internal supports to hold up the roof, sometimes enclosed by timber stockades. This type of architecture is not wasteful when trees can regenerate naturally, but when animals prevent regrowth, and a swelling population makes increasing inroads on woodlands for building materials and farm land, the supply of mature trees eventually fails to meet the growing demand for timber.

Where browsing animals were not allowed to venture into woods, many varieties of tree, once cut down, would not die. The stumps sprouted shoots which grew into a crown of new trunks, and this formed the basis of a system of woodland management known as coppicing. When eight or ten years old such small trees could be cut as roundwood poles for fuel, fence posts, hurdle screens or other needs. Meanwhile, the coppice stool would continue to sprout new growth and would eventually, if left alone, form a circle of individual standard trees which could be felled, when mature, for building timber.

Although the crisis would have come at different times in different places, it was ultimately inevitable that building techniques would have to adapt to the materials available. Distinct changes can be detected during the 1st millennium BC. Palisades were replaced by earthworks or stone walls around settlements; in houses, long timbers were still used for the roof, but smaller buildings with walls of coppice poles, stone or turf were built which did not require roof supports. Lavish use of scarce timber resources under such circumstances, for example on larger buildings, would be an indication of the wealth and power of the individual.

During this same period, the introduction of a greater range of iron tools helped farmers to clear larger areas and farm them more effectively, and as the numbers of remaining standard trees dwindled, the need for positive management of the woodlands would have become more urgent. Although profligate use of the woodland can be seen as a waste in retrospect, the process was gradual, and changes were not noticeable within a particular generation. Even so, there is evidence of woodland management, in the form of coppicing, in Upper Eskdale during the *Iron Age*. Further graphic evidence of this practice was also found at Carlisle (Cumbria), where the waterlogged remains of the Roman fort were excavated in the 1970-80s and dated by *dendrochronology* to 72-73AD. Here Roman troops used huge numbers of standard trees for timber, and thousands of smaller coppice trees for lighter construction. The Borders forts at *Trimontium*, Oakwood, Lyne, and other smaller posts would also have had a similar impact on their surroundings, but if managed wisely the woods could have recovered.

Pollen studies from such sites as Yetholm Loch and Sourhope (Morebattle) indicate that these practices were not successful in stopping extensive woodland clearance and show a clear pattern of deforestation throughout Southern Scotland and Northern England during this period. The geographical extent of known prehistoric settlements and their field systems indicates that by the middle of the 1st millennium AD much of south-eastern Scotland had been subjected to considerable clearance, but the scarcity of such remains in the Ettrick and Yarrow valleys suggests that medieval hunting forests here and possibly elsewhere may have been relics of woodland which escaped the more general level of clearance in early times *(fig.16)*.

Effects of Woodland Clearance

Trees have an important relationship with the soils on which they grow. Their leaf litter breaks down to release nutrients which are important for the maintenance of soil structure and fertility, and which provide food for the trees themselves (as well as for crops grown on the same ground after woodland clearance). These nutrients are dissolved in ground water and carried up into the trees, where the water evaporates in the process known as

transpiration (a fully grown oak tree can release many gallons of water a day from its leaves in this way), and this helps to drain the soil. Clearance of trees to produce arable fields or grazing effectively halts this process, with the result that the fertile *brown earths* of woodland break down into acid heath soils (*podsols*), for example at Harlaw Muir (West Linton) and on Greenlaw Moor.

Heather, which gives Rubers Law and the Eildon Hills their distinctive hues, is a hardy plant which can grow on poor soils and in the shade of trees. With the removal of tree cover, heather moorland developed in many places, particularly in uplands. These areas were, however, susceptible to invasion by grasses, particularly on the Cheviot Hills, and heather is now an indication of where the poorest soils exist.

This process has been recognised on hunter-gatherer sites, as well as on early farming settlements where the nutrition of the soil has been transferred into food crops and lost from the land. Increased ground water, no longer taken up by trees, may accelerate leaching. Leaching is a natural process which washes minerals held in the soil deeper into the ground where they can form hard *pans* and impede drainage even on porous soils. Waterlogging follows which leads to peat formation, and can cause soil erosion. On some Borders hills blanket peat as much as 4 metres (13ft) in depth has formed over thousands of years, particularly during cooler and wetter climatic conditions.

Major soil erosion took place in the mid-3rd millennium BC, probably due to increased rainfall, and again in the second half of the 1st millennium BC due to a widespread increase in agricultural activity. Some of the farms of this period are adjacent to blocks of narrow terracing, which although often presumed to be Anglian or Medieval in date, may have been developed in the late prehistoric period to keep soil from being washed away.

At some point in the first few centuries AD agricultural activity finally shifted away from the upland areas. These areas were now given over to rough pasture and the valley floors and low-lying areas have remained the focus of arable activity since.

Extinctions and Introductions

Whereas climate has had a fundamental influence on what varieties of plants and animals could live in the Borders, people have not only altered the balance of plants and the habitats of animals, but have killed off some British species entirely.

The principal evidence for different animal species comes from surviving body parts, particularly bones and shells, but some creatures have also left traces on plant remains, such as insect damage and tooth marks. Animal remains are scarce, particularly in acid soils, but bones sometimes survive, even a few from earlier *interglacial* periods. These show that prehistoric people lived alongside creatures which are now extinct, as well

as others which survive today, either in Britain or elsewhere. The list of species, and when they lived, grows as more evidence is found.

Leopard (*Panthera pardus*) and hippopotamus (*Hippopotamus amphibius*) bones show that in the period before the last Ice Age the British climate was significantly warmer than at the present day. Different types of animal were able to tolerate the cold conditions which followed, but by 9,000BC many of these were extinct (*fig.22*).

An abundance of wild creatures colonised the developing forests, (*fig.24*) but others such as reindeer (*Rangifer tarandus*) and wild horse (*Equus* sp.) were unable to adapt to the loss of their more open habitat. These, with elk (*Alces alces*) and lynx (*Felis lynx*) had probably been hunted to extinction by the arrival of the first farmers. The *aurochs* (wild ox) survived longer, but is unlikely to have survived into the 1st millennium BC.

Beaver (*Castor fiber*), "Caledonian" (brown) bear (*Ursos arctos*), wolf (*Canis lupus*), and wild boar (*Sus scrofa*) survived in remote areas or in special hunting reserves into historic times before they too were eventually killed off.

Some of these animals have left remains in Borders peat bogs: mammoth (*Mammuthus primigenius*) from Eyemouth, giant deer (*Megaloceras giganteus*) from Coldingham, wild boar from Coldstream. Bones of an *aurochs*

British mammals: extinctions and introductions

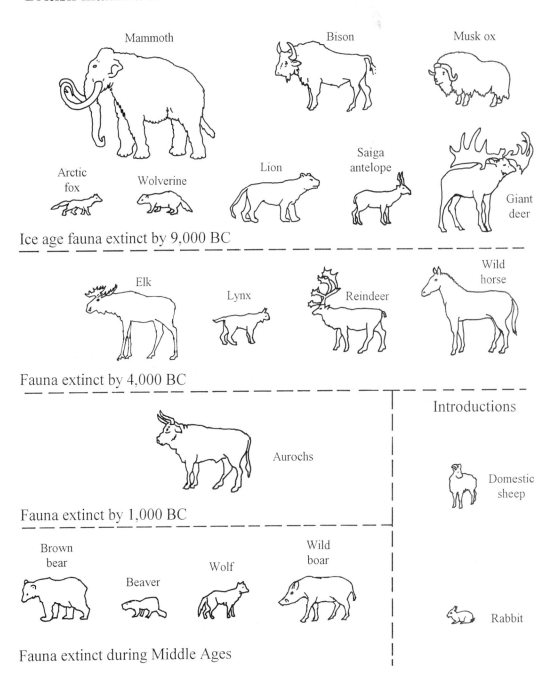

Mammoth

Bison

Musk ox

Arctic fox

Wolverine

Lion

Saiga antelope

Giant deer

Ice age fauna extinct by 9,000 BC

Elk

Lynx

Reindeer

Wild horse

Fauna extinct by 4,000 BC

Introductions

Aurochs

Domestic sheep

Fauna extinct by 1,000 BC

Brown bear

Beaver

Wolf

Wild boar

Rabbit

Fauna extinct during Middle Ages

Fig.22 *Changes in climate and habitat, and the attention of hunters have caused the disappearance of different mammal species from Britain, whereas others have been introduced. The larger, more widely occurring mammals are shown here.*

Fig.23 *The bone structure of Soay sheep is identical to examples of domesticated animals found on prehistoric farming settlements in Britain. Sheep are native to Asia, and are believed to have been introduced into Europe by early farmers.*

Natural Arrivals

- **Aurochs (wild ox)** (*Bos primigenius*).
- **Badger** (*Meles meles*).
- **Beaver** (*Castor fiber*).
- **Brown bear** (*Ursus arctos*).
- **Brown Hare** (*Lepus capensis*).
- **Common Shrew** (*Sorex araneus*).
- **Elk** (*Alces alces*).
- **Fox** (*Vulpes vulpes*).
- **Hedgehog** (*Erinaceus europeus*).
- **Marten** (*Martes martes*).
- **Mole** (*Talpa europea*).
- **Otter** (*Lutra lutra*).
- **Polecat** (*Putorius putorius*).
- **Red Deer** (*Cervus elaphus*).
- **Roe Deer** (*Capreolus capreolus*).
- **Stoat** (*Mustela erminea*).
- **Weasel** (*Mustela nivalis*).
- **Wild Boar** (*Sus scrofa*).
- **Wildcat** (*Felis silvestris*).
- **Wolf** (*Canis lupes*).
- **Woodmouse** (*Apodemus silvaticus*).

Fig.24 *Before 7,000BC, when a land bridge from the continent still existed many mammals reached Britain on their own.*

(fig.8) from Synton Moss (Selkirk) have been dated to the 4th millennium BC, and birch wood felled by a beaver from West Morriston (Earlston) appears to be even older. Red deer (*Cervus elaphus*) bones have been found in many bogs, although the species is no longer resident in the Borders.

By the time that Britain became an island once again, in the 7th millennium BC, most of the species represented in the British Isles today were present. The main exceptions are those with a different environmental background which have been introduced since then and have managed to adapt. The chief of these is the sheep, which is believed to be descended from the Asiatic mouflon or Urial and was introduced, probably along with domesticated varieties of cattle, pigs and goats as early as the 4th millennium BC as part of the farming revolution *(figs.22 & 23)*.

In addition to livestock, early farmers also introduced cereals: the first cereal crops were primitive varieties of wheat and barley developed from wild grasses which are native to modern Iraq and neighbouring countries. Along with cereals came some weeds such as poppies (*Papaver* sp.) and corn-cockle (*Agrostemma githago*), which also originate in the Middle East. Other *flora*, such as plantains (*Plantago* sp.), mugwort (*Artemisia vulgaris*) and shepherd's purse (*Capsella bursa-pastoris*) were originally arctic plants living in the *tundra* of late-glacial Britain. The seeds of these plants had survived the millennia of the *wildwood*, where there was insufficient light for them to grow, and found a new lease of life as weeds when the tree cover was removed by early farmers.

The full range of plants brought in by early farmers is not yet known, and some, such as oats and rye may have been introduced later as outside contacts developed and there was significant expansion in agriculture and population. Increased sea trade with the continent during the *Iron Age* and Roman periods brought ships to Britain, and rodents living on board came ashore and moved inland. Mice (*Mus* sp.) were living in Dorset (England) in the 1st millennium BC, but the first evidence of black rat (*Rattus rattus*), originally from

Roman Introductions

PLANTS

● **Artichoke** (*Cynara scolymus*)

● **Asparagus** (*Asparagus officinalis*)

● **Black Mulberry** (*Morus nigra*)

● **Broad bean** (*Vicia faba*)

● **Cabbage** (*Brassica oleracea*)

● **Cucumber** (*Cucumis sativus*)

● **Eating Apple** (*Malus pumila*)

● **Garlic** (*Allium sativa*)

● **Leek** (*Allium cepa*)

● **Onion** (*Allium porrum*)

● **Sweet Chestnut** (*Castanea sativa*)

ANIMALS

● **Edible Dormouse** (*Muscardinus avellanarius*)

● **Pheasant** (*Phasianus colchinus*)

● **Rabbit?** (*Oryctolagus cuniculus*)

Fig.25 The Romans introduced new species of plants and animals as a source of food.

southern India, comes from York in the 3rd century AD. The more common brown rat (*Rattus norvegicus*) did not arrive in this country from eastern Europe until the 18th century.

It was the Romans, however, who introduced the largest number of plant and animal species into the country as part of the Romanisation of British culture (especially food: *fig.25*). Some of the animals must have escaped and started colonies, although pheasants (*Phasianus colchinus*) and rabbits (*Oryctolagus cuniculus*) have not left traces of significant numbers until more were imported by the Normans. Plants spread far more easily and, in addition to such food varieties as cabbage and onion, many herbs and flowering plants were grown by the Romans.

Quarrying and Mineral Exploitation

The mineral resources of the Borders include metallic ores, stone, sand and gravel, and clay. In the wooded landscape settled by hunter-gatherers such resources would be most easily identified where vegetation was scant, as at the sea coast, along the courses of rivers and streams, and as outcrops and unstable screes in the hills, such as Wood Hill (Newlands) and Clashpock Rig (Stobo) where bands of *chert* were worked. Elsewhere pebbles of workable stone, such as flint or *agate* from stream beds or beaches would have been the main sources from which hunter-gatherers and early farmers made tools (*fig.26*). Longer-range contacts after c.4000BC saw flint imported from Yorkshire, and stone axes brought from the English Lake District to augment local materials.

National Museums of Scotland

Fig.26 *Early farmers used varied sources of stone. These finds from West Linton include two flint knives (right and left), a small core of agate, and a chert flake. © The Trustees of the National Museums of Scotland 1997.*

Early evidence that stone was quarried is surprisingly scarce. Burial cairns may have been built of stones or boulders turned up during cultivation, or collected from river beds, although standing stones or slabs of rock used in burial *cists* are more likely to have been deliberately levered from exposed bedrock. Association of burial sites with cultivation in this way may also be reflected in the construction of earthen barrows, which often used turf stripped from a large area. Turf-stripping was part of the normal process of arable development, and it would be surprising if the opportunity to cultivate ground prepared in this way was ignored.

Large earthworks were constructed by quarrying material from pits or ditches and heaping it up in banks or mounds. At first this treatment was confined to ceremonial and funerary monuments, but was extended to boundaries and settlement enclosures in the 1st millennium BC, by which time stone was coming into use for domestic building as timber became less abundant. A great deal of time and energy was required to quarry, transport and place the large stones used in such sites as the fort on Peniel Heugh (Crailing), the broch at Edin's Hall (Duns), or the circular building at Whitrighill (Mertoun) *(Plate 12)*. Outcrops would be the first to be quarried, and field surfaces must still have been the principal source of stone for walls and enclosures.

The first major quarrying was carried out by the Roman army in the construction of their strategic road network. This is seen very clearly along *Dere Street*, which in many places is flanked by the quarry pits dug to obtain stone for the road *(Plate 13)*.

Stone was quarried and dressed for buildings in the forts, and the easily worked Old Red Sandstone was particularly sought for the fine detail needed for windows, doorways and inscriptions. Gravel from the River Tweed was used to construct the streets in and around the fort at *Trimontium*. Limestone for mortar is scarce in the Borders, and Roman builders may have used other sources, such as clay, to bond stonework together.

The rivers, lochs and glacial deposits of the region also provided clay, which was used by early farming communities (c.4,000BC onwards) to make pottery vessels, some of the finest of which are the decorated funerary vessels that were placed in many of the burials of these people *(Plate 11)*. Clay was also used in conjunction with frames of woven willow (*wattle and daub*) in building, and at *Trimontium* clay *bat* (unfired brick) was used on stone foundations for military buildings.

Metals which occur in the Borders include lead, silver, copper, iron and gold. It is not known to what extent these were exploited by early settlers, as later mining has obliterated most traces. Many of these ores are found in the north-west part of the region around Carlops and West Linton where there are copper, lead and silver deposits, and the best evidence for prehistoric 'mining' has been recovered from this area, where a necklace made up of beads of lead and *cannel coal* (shale) was found in a cemetery of early farmers at West Water Reservoir. This find, the earliest use of lead so far recognised in Britain, was made within two miles of the medieval lead and silver mines at Siller Holes. Lead may also have been worked in the Manor valley from early times. The importance of Edin's Hall, where a huge late *Iron Age* stone *broch* tower dominated the settlement, may have been due in part to a nearby source of copper. Although gold occurs in the Yarrow Valley, evidence of settlement there is sparse, and it may not have been exploited before medieval times. If the location of other metal deposits was known to the prehistoric settlers, it is likely that they exploited them.

Coal deposits can be found near the Berwickshire coast and around West Linton, but although the Romans used coal there is no evidence that it was mined in the Borders until the middle ages. As with so many of the mineral sources in the region, more recent large scale exploitation has obscured any evidence of early workings.

Early Settlers in the Borders

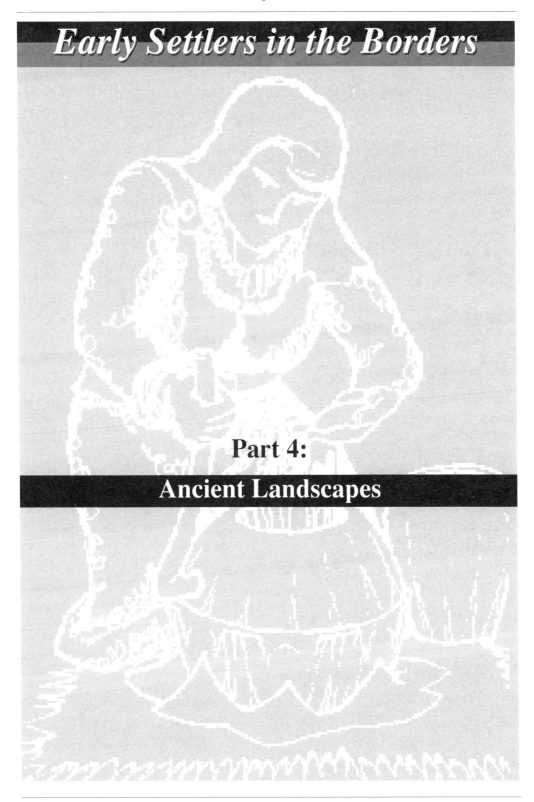

Part 4:

Ancient Landscapes

Underlying rock structure, shaped by ice and water, and the effects of human settlement have produced the present landscape of the Borders. These have determined also where, how, and in what form archaeological remains have survived. Physical destruction has taken place through colossal bulldozing effects of ice sheets, erosion by streams and rivers, fragmentation by roots of plants, and ploughing and quarrying of older sites from early times to the present day. Chemistry of the soil, derived largely from underlying geology, has caused bones and metalwork to dissolve, and drainage of wetlands has caused destruction of organic remains which waterlogged conditions had long preserved.

In spite of these factors the Borders contain some of Britain's best preserved ancient landscapes, and the themes dealt with in earlier chapters can, to some extent, be drawn together by examination of several specific sites, as follows.

The Hunter-Gatherer Phase (c.8,000BC-4,000BC)

Hunter-gatherers were dependent on wild plants and animals for food, clothing and shelter, and their *bands* shifted camp with relative frequency as they exhausted local resources, so that small numbers of people ranged widely across the landscape. Their tools were an improvement on earlier forms, but were still of stone or bone.

Although we may underestimate the extent to which hunters searched the uplands, as their camps sites may lie hidden under hill grazing, the Rotten Bottom bow shows that they climbed up to the tree line in search of game. Most known camp sites occupy attractive locations on gravel river terraces or beside lochs, convenient for travel by canoe, and ideal for catching fish, water fowl or larger animals coming to drink.

Camp sites are identified from scatters of discarded chippings and occasional finished stone tools *(fig.13)*. Rocks such as *chert* were used in the western hills, but a greater variety is found in the lower river valleys of the north-east where *erratic* pebbles can be found in glacial *till* and on coastal beaches. Unusually large concentrations have been found at the junctions of the Tweed with the Ettrick and Teviot and suggest that such places may have had a special significance, perhaps as central base camps or meeting places.

The Borders landscape is now very different, and nowhere do the mixed woodlands of the early post-glacial period survive, nor does extensive commercial forestry recreate them. Only on the coast may we look at cliffs which are little altered since those times, and where early settlers may have trapped birds, collected eggs, and fished from the shore *(Plate 1)*.

The Early Farming Phase (c.4,000BC-2,000BC)

Early farmers continued to depend on stone for tool making, although metals were known by the close of the period, and the more settled life style led to an increase in population. Hunter-gatherer *bands* developed into more settled *tribes* of early farmers, which in turn evolved into *chiefdoms* during this phase.

Houses have not yet been found in the Borders, but could have included both rectangular log-cabin types, and the circular forms which came to dominate later prehistoric settlements. The communal tombs of *tribal* groups, and the individual burials characteristic of the *chiefdom* stage of development still cluster

on the hills around the river valleys which would still have been the main lines of communication. These people worked together to build ceremonial monuments which have left clear traces, and the best concentration of such sites is at Lyne in Peeblesshire.

The Lyne Ceremonial Complex

The junction of the Lyne Water and the Tweed was a place of special importance, *(fig.27)* since it was accessible from the

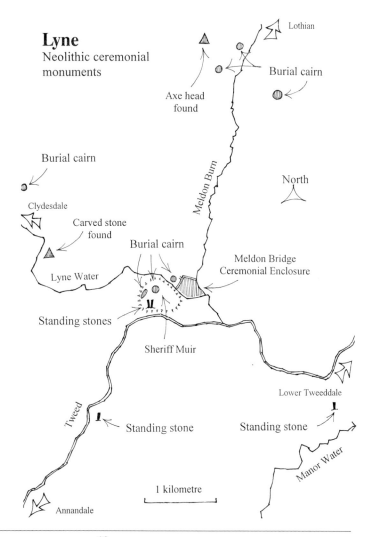

Fig.27 The junction of the Lyne Water and the River Tweed was a convenient place for early farming communities to assemble on special occasions; this is suggested by archaeological sites which would have been central to religious ceremonies and important funerals.

direction of the Pentlands and West Lothian in the north-west, Clydesdale *via* ia the Biggar Gap and the upper Tweed in the south-west, East Lothian *via* the Meldon Burn in the north, and the lower Tweed basin in the east.

On the south bank of the Lyne Water, and west of the Tweed, is the elevated plateau of Sheriff Muir (Stobo). Aerial photographs show that a *long barrow*, a 4th millennium BC communal tomb of the *tribal* stage, may have existed here. The plateau also contains two standing stones and the site of at least two cairns, probably from the more developed *chiefdom* stage.

Between the north side of Lyne Water and the mouth of the Meldon Burn is a level promontory of 8ha (20acres) which began as an open site in the earlier 3rd millennium BC, but was later enclosed by large posts to form a monumental stockade 600m (1,969ft) long and 3-4m (10-12ft) high, entered by a wide passage 25m (83ft) long. This site was excavated in 1974-75, prior to realignment of the A72 road, when cremation deposits and other 'ritual' features, were found along with apparently domestic remains. Whether the site saw long-term occupation, or was the scene of periodic gatherings is not known.

This ritual activity is strongly localised, and although relatively few burials are known from the district, a grave rich in jet ornaments *(Plate 14)*, and characteristic of early *chiefdom* society, was found in the nearby Harehope Cairn.

The geographical importance of this place, which enabled it to operate as a focus for people from further afield, is emphasised by its central position relative to the *hillforts* of later farmers, and to two successive Roman forts and associated temporary camps which were constructed at the mouth of the Lyne valley. For similar geographical reasons Sheriff Muir was also the traditional assembly place of the Peeblesshire Militia in the late 18th century.

Elsewhere in the Borders sites of early farmers are also mainly ritual or funerary *(fig.14)*. Other large monuments, mostly *henges*, have existed beside rivers at Sprouston and Ancrum, and on higher ground at Channelkirk, although all have been reduced by cultivation. At Mellerstain a *henge* forms part of a ritual alignment with three standing stones on Brotherstone Hill. Smaller scale ceremonies would be associated with burial mounds, and prominent *cairns* are features of the landscape on the Dirrington Laws (Greenlaw and Longformacus) and near Cheviot summit. A small cemetery of stone *cists* from West Water Reservoir has been reconstructed at West Linton.

Developed Farming Communities (c.2,000BC-79AD)

The *chiefdom* societies which had developed during the early farming period continued to grow in the 2nd and 1st millennia BC, assisted by wider use of metal tools, at first bronze, and after c.650BC, iron. Further woodland clearance took place, but although various attempts

The Eildon Hills

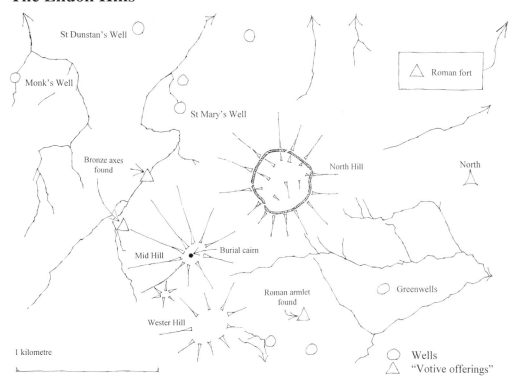

St Dunstan's Well

Monk's Well

St Mary's Well

Roman fort

Bronze axes
found

North Hill

North

Mid Hill

Burial cairn

Greenwells

Roman armlet
found

Wester Hill

1 kilometre

Wells
"Votive offerings"

Fig.28 *Prehistoric and Roman finds made around the base of the three Eildon Hills, and several holy wells suggest that they had a special significance in the landscape, just as they have a place in folklore. The largest hillfort in Scotland occupies North Hill, and may have been a centre for folk gatherings rather than a permanently occupied settlement.*

were made to colonise the uplands, farming was more easily sustained in the lowlands. Open settlements, palisaded sites and fortified farms were the basis of much of this expansion. Characteristic of the later stages of this period are *hillforts*, of which Eildon Hill North is by far the largest. These are symptomatic of insecurity, and it is significant that they were succeeded at Dreva Craig and elsewhere by settlements which in themselves were not designed as strong points. Even at Edin's Hall most of the settlement was indefensible, although it was dominated by a *broch* of formidable strength.

Eildon Hill North

Early farming communities invested considerable effort in the construction of communal ceremonial monuments at Lyne and elsewhere, and the dispersed communities of the Border hills continued to need places where they could meet and take part in communal activities. *Hillforts* may have served this purpose to some extent, and some may also have been centres for gathering and storing farm produce. The largest, and perhaps the most enigmatic, of the Borders *hillforts* is that on Eildon Hill North *(fig.28)*.

Unlike the isolated peaks of Rubers Law or Black Hill, three peaks occur together to make the Eildon hills the most striking landmark of the Borders. In addition, the hills are centrally situated at the point where after its long and narrow course through the hills Tweeddale opens out to form the rich farmlands of the lower Tweed valley and the Merse. The feeder valleys of Ettrick, Yarrow and Gala Waters merge to the west, Lauderdale joins to the east, and southwards the Ale and Teviot already flow through rolling arable farmland, although the whole landscape would still have retained much mixed forest or scrub by the start of 1st millennium BC. The strategic importance of this position, not just within the Tweed basin, but for long distance communication beyond to north and south, is confirmed by the Roman road, *Dere Street* which passed the hill and crossed the Tweed beside the Roman military base of *Trimontium*.

Finds of bronze axes near the springs at the foot of the Eildons, and several holy wells, are evidence of ritual activity around the hills, and the site on Eildon Hill North should be considered against this background. At 404m (1,325ft) North Hill is not the tallest of the three peaks, but it has a broad and level summit, terraces on its sides, and provides very extensive views across to the hills of Northumberland and Dumfriesshire. Although there could have been as many as three different ramparts around the hill, the most convincing is nearly circular in plan, over 1.6km (1 mile) in circumference, and pierced by five entrances.

Within this rampart at least 290 house platforms are known *(Plate 5)*, and many more are likely to have occupied a large area of level ground on the south side of the hill, where medieval cultivation and tree growth have removed any surface traces. Excavation of two of these features indicates that the hill was occupied as early as the 10th century BC, and may have taken the form of an enormous *unenclosed platform settlement*. It is not known how long after this the rampart was built, nor how it related to hut platforms which were in use in the 1st century AD. At this time, or a little later, a rectangular wooden building inside a small circular ditched enclosure, identified as a Roman signal station or watch tower, was constructed on the summit of the hill.

Eildon Hill North is the largest *hillfort* in Scotland, but its exposed position, remoteness from a water supply and the large number of its hut platforms cast doubt on whether or not it was ever occupied on a permanent basis. The dating evidence suggests that activity began 1,000 years before the *Selgovae*, the people whose capital it has been claimed to be, appear in history. Why so many buildings should have been accommodated is not clear, but platforms were re-used and hundreds of huts could have stood at one time. Not all need have been for human accommodation, for they might have been storage buildings for produce from a wide area. The central position of the site would have been important for any trade or re-distribution of such produce.

Dreva Craig

The valley which joins Tweeddale and Clydesdale narrows at its eastern end and is dominated by Dreva Craig, a knoll 80m (250ft) above the valley floor, and part of a prominent spur of Dreva Hill. The settlements which once existed here occupied a zone between arable cultivation in the valley and pasture for animals on the hill, and this relationship is particularly clear from surviving remains, although no excavations have taken place here *(fig.29)*.

The earliest attempt to settle this exposed ridge may date to the earlier 1st millennium BC, and be represented by traces of two timber round houses which stood outside a banked enclosure north-east of the later occupation. Absence of stone buildings suggests that the settlement was abandoned before use of stone became general on the hill, although lack of success did not discourage medieval farmers from erecting rectangular buildings on this site 2,000 years later.

A strong *hillfort* formed the next stage of occupation, which probably dates to the

middle of the 1st millennium BC. The fort consisted of two concentric enclosures with stone walls up to 3.5m (11ft) in thickness, and where steep slopes did not provide additional protection, the approaches were obstructed by boulders set in rows, known as *chevaux de frise*. These can still be seen to the south of the fort, but on the north side most of the stones have been cleared to make way for later settlement. Although traces of some small stone round houses can be seen in the interior, these may have been built from stones taken from the fort walls after the defences had fallen into disuse.

The final stage of occupation, in the late 1st millennium BC, is represented by two groups of stone courts, some containing visible remains of circular buildings, which cluster beneath the ramparts of the earlier fort. The larger of these groups extends along the upper limit of the former arable fields, which by this stage had been divided from hill grazing by a stone head dyke. From this head dyke stone walls extend down the slope to divide areas of cultivation, and to define a drove road, which linked the hill with the valley below. The walls here would have been particularly important to ensure that animals did not stray onto growing crops while on their way to or from their watering places on the valley floor.

The sequence at Dreva, although not yet confirmed by excavation, runs from unenclosed timber buildings, *via* a stone fort, to nucleated settlement and field

Dreva

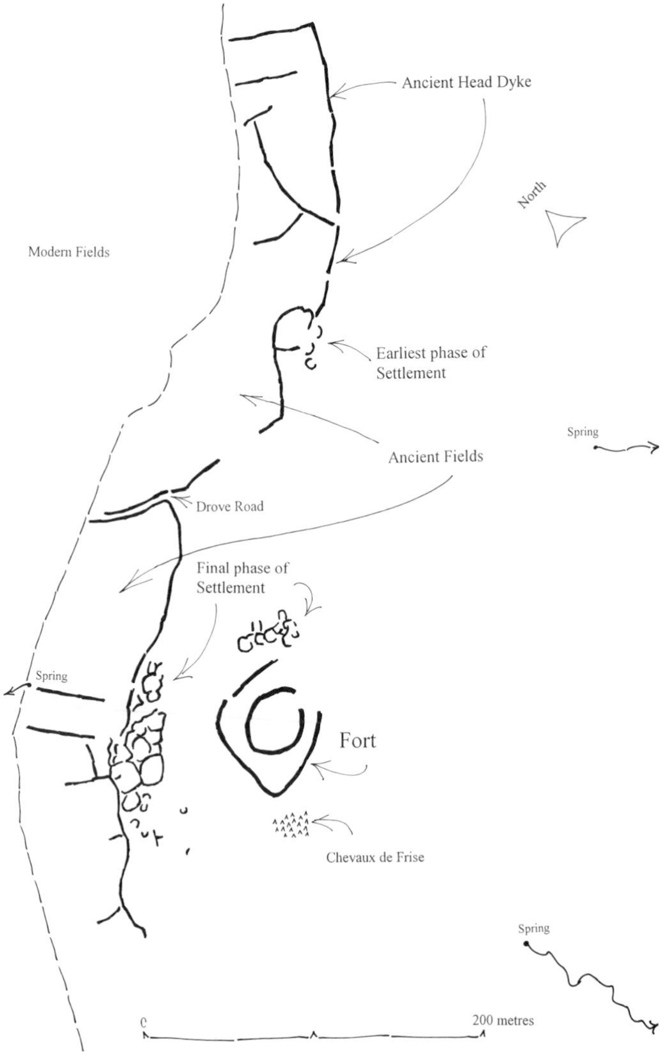

Ancient Head Dyke

North

Modern Fields

Earliest phase of
Settlement

Spring

Ancient Fields

Drove Road

Final phase of
Settlement

Spring

Fort

Chevaux de Frise

Spring

0   200 metres

Fig.29 *The extent of arable land at Dreva has altered very little since the 1ˢᵗ millennium BC when the head dyke between cultivated fields and hill grazing was only marginally higher up the slope than today. A series of settlements were constructed at the junction of the two zones, and these reflect a wider pattern of changing settlement types.*

system clearly delineated in stone. The change in building materials would reflect both technological advances, with increased availability of iron tools during this period, and the severe impact of farming communities on the ecology of the district, which caused woodland shrinkage, leaving field systems and grazing around the settlements, with mixed woodland or scrub further off.

The *hillfort* reflects the uncertainties of the times, which may have been caused in part by population pressures, and later

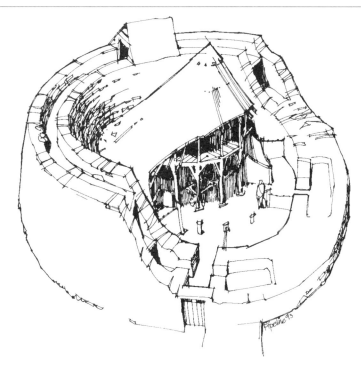

Fig.30 *This cut-away reconstruction drawing of Edin's Hall broch by Dave Pollock shows how the traditional round house was developed into a structure of great strength. The owner of this building would have enjoyed great prestige in the Borders. © Crown copyright by courtesy of Historic Scotland.*

settlements appear to reflect changed circumstances, perhaps with power struggles resolved through the emergence of strong regional leadership.

Edin's Hall

Edin's Hall does not possess the detail of agricultural landscape which can be traced at Dreva, but it is remarkable for its structural remains, which set it apart among Borders settlements as a place of exceptional prestige. Even its association with Edin, or Wooden (an alternative spelling) suggest that folklore links it to the Germanic god Woden or Odin, or possibly even to King Edwin of *Northumbria.*

The settlement is situated on the northern flank of Cockburn's Law, on a steep bluff overlooking the Whiteadder Water. The site developed from a minor *hillfort* into a highly prestigious settlement centred on a large *broch*, and this may have been due in part to the existence of copper ore at Elba, 1km to the east, where mine adits survive from more recent times. The *broch* was cleared of debris in the 19th century and no other excavations took place until 1996, when some trenches were opened to assess the extent of damage caused to the monument by rabbits.

The fort is represented by an oval enclosure defended by substantial banks with external ditches, double ramparts being provided on all but the river side, where the steep slope provided its own defence *(Plate 15)*. The defended area was a little larger than the fort at Dreva Craig, and measured 135m by 75m (443ft by 246ft), with its entrance at the eastern end, but no trace can now be seen of any internal buildings of this phase, which dates to around the middle of the 1st millennium BC.

Development of a more significant place in regional society is represented by the next phase, which began toward the end of the 1st millennium BC and continued into the early centuries AD. This phase saw dramatic reorganisation of the interior of the fort, and the replacement of the earlier ramparts, now largely redundant, by a complex of stone walled enclosures and buildings. Under these new arrangements the *broch* formed the focal point of the settlement and was reached from the east by a path which led between walled courts containing smaller circular buildings.

Today the *broch* consists of a massive drystone wall 5-6m (16-20ft) thick and in places almost 2m (6ft) high, which encloses a circular area 17m (55ft) in diameter, that is larger, than any other *broch*. The original height of the wall is not known, but examples elsewhere, and a stone stair in one of several chambers built in the thickness of the wall indicate that there was at least one upper storey. The general shape resembles the traditional round house, and the *broch* should be seen as a very special

development of that building form, and one which implies exceptionally high status of the owner *(fig.30)*. The high stone walls, probably with a wall walk, made the *broch* secure from attack, and entry was solely *via* a narrow passage rebated for a door. Only two other *brochs* are known in the Borders, both near Galashiels, but a related structure known as a *dun* survives near Tweedsmuir. Although Edin's Hall could have been occupied by Anglian settlers - perhaps helping to explain the name - the settlement shows no sign of characteristic rectangular buildings, nor have excavations provided any evidence of later occupation.

Roman Remains

Although they represent a temporary intrusion into the region by a foreign imperial power, which remained a neighbour for more than 300 years, the military works left by Roman soldiers are of particular interest in their own right and for the complete contrast which they provide with the native remains.

Pennymuir Camps and Dere Street

What, if any, resistance was encountered by the Roman army in their advance northwards into the Border hills is not recorded. Their victory at *Mons Graupius* c.AD83 enabled them to consolidate, in due course, their conquests with a legionary fortress at Inchtuthil (near Perth) linked to the fortress at *Eburacum* (York) by a new strategic road (later known as *Dere Street*), and with a series of smaller garrisons

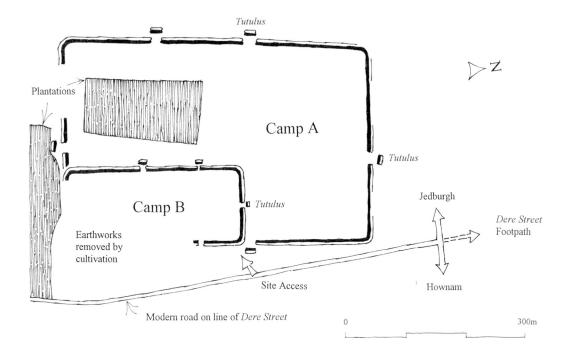

Fig.31   *The Roman camps at Pennymuir.*

which made use of existing native tracks and built new roads as needed and as resources allowed.

Dere Street is well preserved where it crosses the Cheviot Hills, and near Soutra on the Lammermuir Hills. Where later use has not resulted in changes it takes the form of a central embankment with ditches on either side, flanked in turn by small quarry pits where suitable stone was available to surface the road itself. Particularly well preserved quarry pits can be seen on the stretch between Pennymuir and Whitton Edge in Oxnam parish *(Plate 13)*.

This road remained in use, whether or not the area was under Roman rule, and was a major invasion route on those occasions when the Imperial forces were brought north of Hadrian's Wall. The places where such forces stopped along the road are still marked by the sites of tented camps, which the soldiers enclosed with temporary earthwork fortifications. The best preserved are at Pennymuir, where the strategic road, having followed the heights of the Cheviot plateau, crosses the valley of the Kale Water.

Although two of the four camps at Pennymuir have been substantially levelled, two are exceptionally well preserved *(fig.31)*. Camp (A) is the largest in the group and encloses 17ha (42acres), which would have been sufficient to house two legions totalling about ten thousand men. It is clearly bounded by a rampart and ditch except in the south-east corner where later cultivation has levelled the earthworks. Camp B lies within the south-east portion of Camp A and shared the larger camp's defences on the south and east sides.

These camps were constructed to a basic pattern which had been tried and tested on many campaigns. Soldiers arrived at the site to find a camp marked out by their surveyors, and space allotted to the army staff, the different units, and the supply column. The army carried the tools to clear the site and construct a fortified enclosure, and as each unit arrived on site soldiers were allocated sections of the perimeter to fortify, which they did by digging a ditch or *fossa*, building the upcast into a bank or *vallum*, and raising a temporary fence on top. Regular tent lines were pitched inside the camp, and the weakest points of the perimeter - the entrances - were provided with movable barriers and additional earthwork defences for security. At Pennymuir these earthworks took the form of short traverses, or *tutuli*, in front of the entrance, and several can still be seen.

The need for such fortifications amid a potentially hostile population is emphasised by the large number of native settlements in the neighbourhood, including several *hillforts*, of which that on Woden Law (Oxnam) was particularly well placed to interrupt the flow of traffic along the road. At this time the landscape would have contained many more trees, and the poor grazing of today is largely the product of later processes.

Forts were intended to be permanent, and were equipped with buildings rather than tents, and enclosed by more robust fortifications. The most important military post, (*Trimontium*) guarded the crossing of the Tweed at Newstead, but few features can now be discerned on the ground, although a monument now marks the site of the fort and recent excavations of an embanked enclosure outside the fort's north-east corner suggest that it was an amphitheatre for the entertainment of the garrison.

The best preserved fort in the Borders is near Lyne Kirk in Peeblesshire *(Plate 6)*. Here much has been levelled by ploughing, but extensive remains of the fort ramparts still remain on a bluff overlooking a bend in the river.

Anglian Settlement

Although many Borders villages are ancient, and such names as Midlem (*Middle-ham; ham* = settlement) and Ednam (*Eden-ham*) date from the *Early Historic* period of the 6th or 7th century AD, surprisingly few settlements of that period are known from archaeological remains.

Of those which are, the most extensive is known only from aerial photographs of

Sprouston
Anglian Settlement

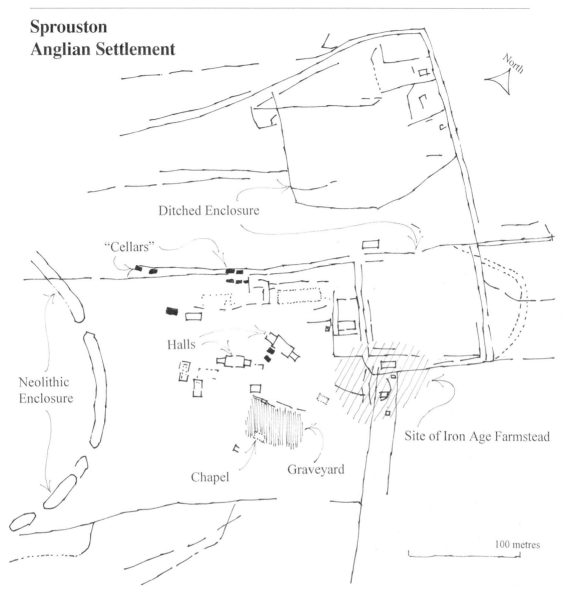

Fig.32 *The Anglian settlement at Sprouston is known entirely from aerial photographs, and may have been an aristocratic manor established in a traditional meeting place which had been marked earthworks since the 3rd millennium BC.*

cropmarks, is located on raised ground beside the River Tweed near Sprouston in Roxburghshire, and covers an area of at least 16ha (40acres) *(fig.32)*. One reason for the choice of this site may have been the presence of prehistoric ceremonial earthworks, which could have retained some tradition of special importance with which new, Anglian landlords could identify.

Anglian use of the site is represented by a complex of features which represent

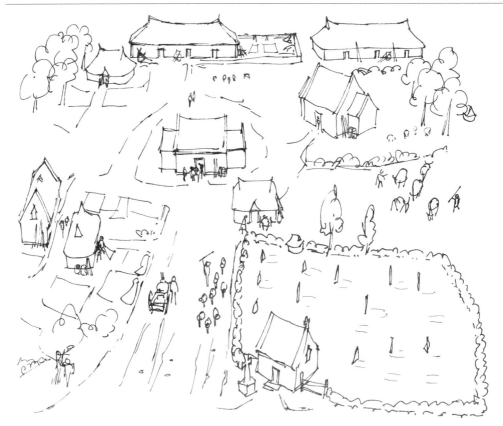

Fig.33 *Reconstruction of the Anglian settlement at Sprouston, based upon the cropmark information shown in Fig.30.*

enclosures, buildings and other components of the settlement. Buildings, sometimes of more than one room, are represented by wall slots, post holes, and even the shallow cellars (*grubenhäuser*) of rectangular or bow-sided timber buildings (*fig.33*).

These structures are in complete contrast to earlier native round houses, and a building c.30m (100ft) in length is much larger than any buildings constructed by the native British. A distinctive three-room building form, in which the two ends are smaller than the middle room, has also been found at Yeavering 18km (11 miles) away

in Northumberland, where King Edwin of *Northumbria* had a palace in the early 7th century AD, and where they have been interpreted as halls.

Sprouston had a cemetery, for the marks of at least 380 graves can be seen on aerial photographs. The graves were all aligned west-east, which is still normal Christian orientation, and a small building on the south side of the graveyard may have been a chapel or church. The site of Yeavering had a similar cemetery, also associated with a church-like building, but that site also had a pagan temple with evidence of cattle sacrifices. Given the evidence of the cemetery and "church" at Sprouston, the Yeavering temple is a useful reminder that settlers of the *Early Historic* period maintained beliefs in Germanic gods such as Tiwaz, Woden, Thor, Freya (who still give us Tuesday, Wednesday, Thursday and Friday) which were only gradually supplanted as adherence to the new Christian religion gained momentum in King Edwin's reign and afterwards.

The status of the site at Sprouston is not known. If it was the home of an aristocrat, and as such, a centre for social and ceremonial activity then, like Yeavering, the site seems to have been chosen partly for the prehistoric ceremonial earthworks which already marked the place. Some early Christians also deliberately selected places which had a traditional religious importance, albeit pagan, as the site of their monasteries. Until it is examined by excavation this important site provides more questions than answers.

Although the settlements of this period are mostly buried beneath modern villages, the ramparts of 6th century *Colodaesburg*, or fort of Colud still survive on St Abb's Head (Coldingham), on the cliff-top site later used by St Ebba for her monastery. The *orthostatic* walls of Peniel Heugh fort , and Castle Hill (Ancrum) may also have been erected at this time, when their closeness to *Dere Street* gave special strategic importance to the strongholds. In general, however, the dearth of archaeological sites reflects the success of *Early Historic* period settlers, whose villages have developed to form part of the modern settlement pattern.

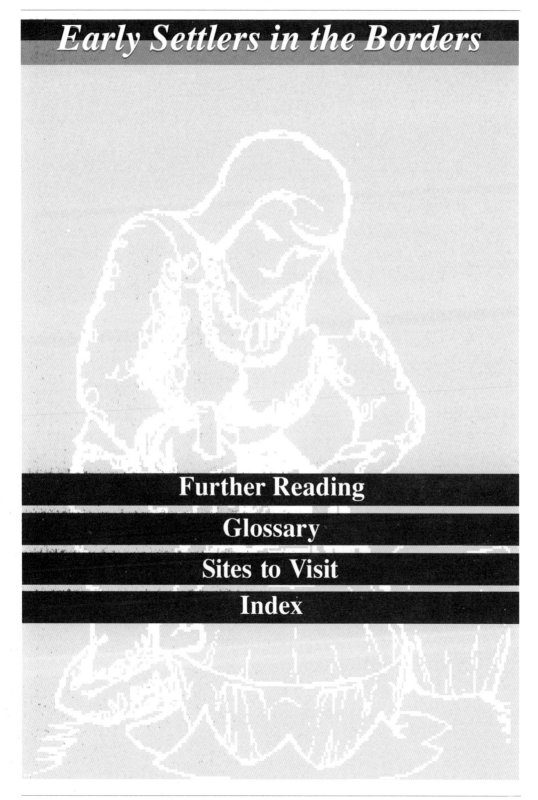

Early Settlers in the Borders

Further Reading

Glossary

Sites to Visit

Index

Further Reading

Ashmore, P J 1996. *Neolithic & Bronze Age Scotland*. Batsford, London.

Baldwin, J R 1985. *Exploring Scotland's Heritage: Lothian and the Borders*, HMSO.

Breeze, D J 1996. *Roman Scotland*. Batsford, London.

McAdam, A D, Clarkson, E N K, & Stone, P 1992. *Scottish Borders Geology, an excursion guide*. Scottish Academic Press, Edinburgh.

Omand, D (ed.) 1995. *The Borders Book*. Birlinn Ltd, Edinburgh.

Pearson, M P 1993. *Bronze Age Britain*. BT Batsford/English Heritage, London.

RCAHMS 1956. *An Inventory of the Ancient and Historic Monuments of Roxburghshire*. HMSO, Edinburgh.

RCAHMS 1957. *An Inventory of the Ancient and Historic Monuments of Selkirkshire*. HMSO, Edinburgh.

RCAHMS 1967. *Peeblesshire; An Inventory of the Ancient Monuments*. HMSO, Edinburgh.

Ritchie, A & Breeze, D J 1991. *Invaders of Scotland*. HMSO, Edinburgh.

Whyte, I 1990. *Edinburgh & the Borders, Landscape Heritage*. David & Charles, London.

Wickham-Jones, C R 1994. *Scotland's First Settlers*. Batsford, London.

Glossary

agate: flinty stone of volcanic origin.

Arthur: heroic leader of British legend.

aurochs: type of wild ox, the ancestor of the domesticated cow. Latin name *Bos primigenius*.

band: small-scale, *egalitarian* social unit, in which status is based upon age and kinship. Such units characteristically live by hunting and gathering.

bat: unfired clay brick.

beaker: type of fine pottery jar, particularly associated with the graves of early *chiefdom* societies from c.2,500BC.

beehive quern: see *quern*.

Beowolf: hero of Germanic legend.

Bernicia: Anglian Kingdom approximating to modern Northumberland.

bog bodies: human remains preserved in peat bogs, and sometimes shown to be victims of human sacrifice.

broch: defensible stone tower, found only in Scotland, and based upon the traditional round house form. Most were built between the 2nd century BC and 2nd century AD.

Bronze Age: phase of *chiefdom* society which followed the introduction of metal working in about 2,500-2,000BC and which lasted until the introduction of iron working in about 650BC.

brown earths: fertile soil type formed in woodland.

caer: *Cumbric* for "fort", equivalent to Latin "*castra*", Old English "*caestr*".

caestr: Old English for "fort", equivalent to Latin "*castra*", Cumbric "*caer*".

cannel coal: dull organic shale which burns with a smoky luminous flame, which was worked into beads and bracelets in the prehistoric period.

Carbon dating: see *half life* and *radiocarbon dating*.

Carboniferous: a geological period dated to between 360 and 290 million years ago.

carnivore: meat eating animal.

Catraeth: Catterick in Yorkshire, Latin name *Catteractonium*. The scene of a battle between the *Goddodin* and the Angles.

chert: type of flint-like rock.

chevaux de frise: literally: "horses of Frisia", so-called because foot soldiers from German Frisia used a barrier of sharpened stakes as a defence against cavalry. The term is applied to any defence, including rows of earth-fast rocks, intended to disrupt an organised attack.

chiefdom: developed society headed by an hereditary chief, in which social rank is determined by kinship to the chief, and so can be inherited rather than earned. *Chiefdoms* developed after c.3,000BC and include the British tribal groups conquered by the Romans, as well as the kingdoms established by the Picts, Scots and Angles.

Chu Chulainn: mythical hero of Irish legend.

cinerary urn: type of large jar, often coarsely decorated, which contained the cremated remains of the dead.

cist: a small burial chamber to contain a single body, and usually made of stone slabs.

Colodaesburg: Anglian settlement (Colod's Fort), located on St Abbs Head.

continental drift: the very slow movement of large land masses across the surface of the globe (see *tectonic plates*).

cord rig: type of prehistoric cultivation akin to modern "lazy beds", consisting of very narrow parallel ridges, generally no more than 1.4m apart.

corrie: place where glaciers formed on mountain sides, now represented as cove-shaped depressions at the heads of valleys.

crinoid: long existinct relative of the star fish and sea urchin, protected by a shell and supported by a stem.

cropmark: discolouration of arable crops due to buried archaeological features, and best seen from the air.

cultivation terraces: stepped farming strips running parallel with the contours.

Cumbric: language of mainland Britain in late prehistoric times, precursor to modern Welsh.

Dalriada: Scottish Kingdom based in Argyle and the Western Isles.

Dark Ages: period of supposed "barbarism" between the end of Roman Britain and the establishment of the Christian kingdoms documented by the Venerable Bede and other writers. Also known as the *Early Historic* period.

Deira: Anglian Kingdom approximating to modern day Yorkshire and County Durham.

Dendrochronology: dating method by which scientists use the growth pattern preserved in annual tree rings to establish the age of ancient timbers.

Dere Street: post-Roman name of the strategic road built in the 1st century AD to the northern frontier from *Eburacum* (York), which became the capital of *Deira.*

Devonian: a geological period dated to between 408 and 360 million years ago.

Din Eiddyn: *Cumbric* for Edinburgh

drumlin: elongated clay hill shaped by a moving glacier..

dun: a stone-built fortified round-house, akin to the *brochs*. Most were built between the 2nd century BC and 2nd century AD.

dyke: geological term for a sheet-like, often vertical, intrusion of igneous rock.

Early Historic Period: the period between the end of Roman Britain and the establishment of stable Christian kingdoms. Also known as the *Dark Ages*.

Eburacum: The Roman capital of *Britannia Inferior* ("Lower Britain"), now York.

egalitarian: social structure in which all individuals are of equal status and which is guided (rather than lead), usually by the elder members of the community (see *bands*).

einkorn: a primitive form of wheat

erratic: any rock which has been removed from its place of origin and deposited by glaciation.

esker: winding gravel ridge deposited by meltwater beneath a glacier.

excarnation: deliberate exposure of a corpse to the elements and predation by animals. Sometimes followed by formal burial at a later date.

faience: an early form of glass which occurs as beads in graves of early *chiefdom* societies from c.2,000BC.

fault: a fracture in the rock along which there has been movement.

flora: "vegetation" (Latin).

food vessel: type of pottery bowl, particularly associated with the graves of early *chiefdom* societies from c.2,500-2,000BC.

fossa: Latin technical term for the ditch enclosing a temporary camp (see also *vallum*).

Gododdin: subject of a British epic poem in which a band of warriors of the *Votadini* (Gododdin) rode from *Din Eiddyn* to *Catraeth* and died there in battle.

graptolite: a primitive marine life form found as fossils in *Ordovician* and *Silurian* rocks.

Grendel: a monster in Germanic folklore, vanquished by *Beowolf*.

grooved ware: a type of decorated pottery associated with early *chiefdom* societies from c.3,000BC.

grubenhäuser: literally "sunken-featured building", being large pits which occur in Anglian settlements and are thought to have underlain wooden houses, to help drainage or act as cellars.

half life: 5,730 years is the rate at which 50% of Carbon-14, which is present in all living things, decays. From this knowledge ancient organic remains can be dated.

ham: Old English word meaning village.

henge: form of circular earthwork erected by early *chiefdom* societies for ceremonial purposes from c.3,000BC. Unlike later fortified sites the ditch runs inside the enclosing bank.

herbivore: plant eating animal.

hillfort: type of fortified site occupying a prominent topographical position, and characteristic of developed *chiefdom* societies.

Holocene: a geological period dated to between 12,000 years ago and the present day.

Iapetus: a prehistoric ocean in which the rocks of the Borders formed in the *Ordovician* and *Silurian* eras.

igneous: (of rock) formed from molten rock (as opposed to water or wind born sediments).

interglacial: warm period between Ice Ages.

interlace: knot designs used in Early Christian art, sometimes incorporating fantastic beasts.

Iron Age: phase of *chiefdom* society following the introduction of iron technology around 650BC, generally seen as ending with Roman conquest, but effectively continuing in areas outside the Roman Province.

isostatic uplift: reaction of *tectonic plates* to the weight loss from melting ice sheets, resulting in raised beaches and coastal platforms.

La Tène: *Iron Age* tradition, especially of metalworking, named after the site of that name in Switzerland.

laccolith: geological term for a lens shaped volcanic intrusion.

Laurentia: ancient supercontinent that was made up of modern day America and Europe.

long barrow: communal burial mound constructed mainly of earth by early farmers.

long cairn: communal burial mound constructed mainly of stones by early farmers.

mantle: the molten core of the Earth on which float *tectonic plates*.

marl: lime-rich clay applied to arable soil to reduce acidity.

matriarch: female head of a family or society.

Merlin: wizard of British legend, reputedly buried at Drumelzier.

mesolithic: literally "Middle Stone Age", the final phase of hunter-gatherer *band* society, which lasted from the end of the last Ice Age until the adoption of farming in c.4,000BC.

microlith: small stone tool used for the points or barbs of composite hunting weapons such as harpoons and arrows.

Mons Graupius: site of the victory in c.AD83, at an unknown location, of Roman forces under C I Agricola over a native army of Caledones under Calgacus

moraine: material deposited by a melting glacier.

neolithic: literally "New Stone Age", the period which saw the introduction of farming c.4,000BC and the development of *tribes* into *chiefdoms*. Adoption of metal-working in c.2,500-2,000BC heralded the end of dependence on stone for everyday tools.

Northumbria: land north of the River Humber, over which Aethelfrith of *Bernicia* established his dominion in the early 7th century AD. His successors extended their power beyond the Forth until Ecgfrith's defeat and death at Nechtanesmere in AD685.

Orans: praying figure (Latin), a subject of Early Christian sculpture.

Ordovician: a geological period dated to between 505 and 438 million years ago.

orthostatic: built from large, upright stone slabs.

palaeolithic: literally "Old Stone Age", the period of human development from the earliest use of stone tools to the end of the last Ice Age.

palynology: study of ancient pollen grains.

pan: hard metallic layers formed in the soil, which impede drainage and root growth, and can be a source of iron ore.

patriarch: male head of a family or social unit.

pen: *Cumbric* for "hill".

pipe: volcanic vent formed from solidified lava.

Pleistocene: a geological period dated to between 2.4 million and 12,000 years ago.

podsols: leached, unfertile soils characteristic of moorland, in which iron pan formations aggravate drainage problems.

quern: stone hand mill for grain. The earliest form, the *saddle quern* was a flat stone on which grain was crushed using a smaller stone; the *rotary*, or *beehive quern* consisted of one circular mill stone on top of another, and grain was fed through a hole in the upper stone (see *fig.9*).

radiocarbon dating: dating technique which estimates the time elapsed since the death of plants or animals by calculating the rate of decay of the radioactive carbon which they contain (see *half life*).

redoubt: earthwork artillery fortification designed to resist attack from all sides.

rotary quern: see *quern*.

saddle quern: see *quern*.

sedimentary: (of rocks) formed as water or wind born deposits.

Selgovae: one of the British *tribes* which inhabited the Southern Uplands in the 2nd century AD, and associated with *Trimontium*.

Silurian: a geological period dated to between 438 and 408 million years ago.

state: class-based society headed by a king or emperor assisted by a centralised bureaucracy.

strata: layers of *sedimentary* rock.

Strathclyde: a British kingdom which occupied the Clyde valley in the *Early Historic Period*.

tectonic plate: landmass, not more than 35km thick under Britain, which floats on the molten core of the earth (*mantle*) and moves at an extremely slow rate (see *continental drift*).

tepee: tent made of animal hides or tree bark over a frame of wooden poles, and used in recent times by hunter-gatherers of North America.

Tertiary: a geological period dated to between 65 million and 2.4 million years ago.

till: glacial deposit commonly known as Boulder Clay.

tilth: soil prepared for sowing with seed.

torc: neck ring, associated with high status.

transpiration: evaporation of water from trees through their leaves.

tref: *Cumbric* for "homestead," or "village".

tribe: group of farming communities organised into a *tribe* and linked by marriage bonds. Status is based on age and ability more than kinship, but clear-cut hierarchies have not formed. Seen as the model for early farming communities from c.4,000BC.

Trimontium: literally "Three Peaks". The Roman name for the military post at Newstead.

tundra: barren arctic landscape where only small, low growing plants, such as mosses and lichens can survive, such as parts of Greenland or Lapland.

tutulus: a short stretch of defensive bank and ditch in front of the gate of a Roman camp.

umiak: skin boat used by Esquimaux.

unconformity: junction between *sedimentary strata* lying on a former land surface, and *strata* below which lie obliquely and may be highly contorted.

unenclosed platform settlement: village or hamlet represented only by house platforms terraced into the hillside.

vallum: Latin technical term for the rampart enclosing a temporary camp (see also *fossa*).

vicus: civilian settlement outside a Roman fort.

Votadini: one of the British tribes which inhabited the Southern Uplands in the 2nd century AD, associated as the *Gododdin* with *Din Eiddyn* in later literature.

wattle and daub: use of woven willow (*wattle*) or similar wands in combination with clay (*daub*) as a building construction.

wildwood: wholly natural woodland unaffected by *neolithic* and later populations.

yurt: portable tent made from felt and wooden poles used by the nomadic peoples of the Mongolian steppes.

zoomorphic: animal-like (especially of metalwork or wood carving).

Sites to Visit

*1   Cardrona Forest Walk,
      Traquair; NT 292 384*

Cardrona Forest is situated on the south side
of the River Tweed approximately 3 miles
east of Peebles. There are parking and
picnic facilities and three waymarked
walks, two of which afford opportunities
to view the remains of an *Iron Age* fort
and the medieval Cardrona Castle.

*2   Chambers Institute, High
      Street, Peebles; NT 253 403*

The museum regularly holds exhibitions
about the culture of the Borders.

*3   Craik Forest, Roberton;
      NT 345 079*

Craik Forest is situated beside the upper
Borthwick Water, approximately 10 miles
south-west of Hawick. There are parking
and picnic facilities, with extensive walks
and cycle routes. Archaeological sites
include the Roman road from Newstead
to Carlisle, small *Iron Age* settlements, and
a carved boulder, the "Loupin' on Stane".

*4   Dere Street, Fala and Soutra;
      NT 402 580*

A well-preserved section of the strategic
Roman road, *Dere Street* is in the care of
Historic Scotland, and can be reached from
the B 6368 road. On a clear day extensive
views northwards can be enjoyed from the
vicinity of Soutra Aisle.

*5   Dreva Craig, Stobo;
      NT 126 353*

On a knoll 1 mile east of Broughton are a
series of well-preserved remains which
represent changing land use in the *Iron
Age*, and include an early settlement, a
hillfort with *chevaux de frise*, and later
settlement with associated fields (*see Part
4*).

*6   Duns Law, Duns;
      NT 785 547*

A path leads north from Castle Street to
the hill known as Duns Law, on which can
be seen an *Iron Age hillfort*. The
occupation of the hill by General Leslie's
army during the First Bishops' War of

1638, has left a *redoubt*, three small circular banks resembling gun emplacements, and the Covenanters' Stone. On the southern slopes of Duns Law are a series of well-preserved *cultivation terraces* which probably date to the medieval period.

7 Edin's Hall Broch, Duns; NT 772 603

The striking gorge cut by the Whitadder Water contains some of the oldest woodland surviving in the Borders, and provides an attractive approach to Edin's Hall *via* Elba footbridge 1 mile to the east. The site is in the care of Historic Scotland and consists of an *Iron Age hillfort*, which was replaced by a large stone *broch* and associated settlement of round houses in walled courts (*see Part 4*). The wildlife of the valley may be enjoyed more fully by an extended walk taking in Abbey St Bathans.

8 Eildon North Hill, Melrose; NT 555 328

The summit of Eildon North Hill is crowned by the largest *hillfort* in Scotland (*see Part 4*). There are over 300 hut circles within the ramparts of this fort, and on the top extensive views may be enjoyed from the site of a Roman watch tower Footpaths which incorporate the hill include the Eildon Walk and St Cuthbert's Way. Volcanic rocks which formed the hills were once quarried between Mid Hill and North Hill, and red grouse live among the heather.

9 Fort Point & Corn Fort, Eyemouth; NT 941 649

Natural coastal promontories provide the sites of the *Iron Age* Corn Fort, and successive 16th century English and French artillery forts on Fort Point. The rugged coast here provides some spectacular views, and is formed of volcanic rocks which now provide nesting places for many sea birds. A longer walk may be enjoyed by following the cliff path to Coldingham.

10 Innerleithen Cross; NT 3320 3695

The decorated shaft base of a *Dark Age* cross now stands against the east wall of Innerleithen Parish Church.

11 Jail & Museum, Castlegate, Jedburgh; NT 648 202

The Victorian prison now contains various exhibits relating to the history of Jedburgh, including finds made during excavations at the Dunion *Iron Age hillfort*.

12 Kirk Hill, St Abbs Head, Coldingham; NT 916 687

To the south of the lighthouse, on Kirk Hill, are the remains of the 6th century Anglian settlement *Colodaesburg* (Colud's Fort) and the later 7th century monastery of St Ebba. A low earthen rampart encloses the summit of the hill, within which are the low rectangular foundations of buildings or halls. Kirk Hill and the adjacent cove of Burnmouth Harbour afford excellent views of the rock formations which make up St Abbs Head and provide an opportunity to see the various sea-birds which make their home on the cliffs.

Access to the site is *via* the Visitors Centre.

13 Lindean Reservoir, Galashiels; NT 503 291

Now a site of great natural importance, and a breeding ground for a variety of birds, this filled-up loch was quarried for *marl* in the 18th century, when bones of *aurochs* were discovered here. In 1904 the site was made into a reservoir to supply nearby villages.

14 Roman Fort, Lyne; NT 188 405

The best preserved Roman fort in the Borders. Although the interior has been cultivated and the rampart has been reduced by ploughing, the ditches can easily be traced on three sides, and the eastern entrance is particularly clear. Access is from the lane leading to Lyne Kirk.

Please note that particular caution should be shown when turning out of the lane back onto the A 72.

15 Priest Hill Forest Walk, Newcastleton; NY 503 877

Facilities include Dykecrofts Information Centre, with an exhibition of forestry past and present. Forest walks around Priest Hill provide an opportunity to examine the remains of an *Iron Age hillfort*, abandoned medieval farmsteads, and take in some fine views of Liddesdale.

16 Peniel Heugh, Crailing; NT 654 262

Peniel Heugh may be reached as one of the network of walks which radiates from Harestanes Countryside Visitor Centre, and includes St Cuthbert's Way and *Dere Street*. The remains of an *Iron Age hillfort* on the summit are in turn overlain by the massive stone walls of what may be a *Dark Age* fort. In the centre of these stands a tall tower begun in 1815 to commemorate the Battle of Waterloo and from the hill top there are extensive all-round views of the Borders.

17 Pennymuir, Oxnam; NT 755 140

The best preserved set of Roman temporary camps in Scotland are set in wild moorland and are overlooked by the *hillfort* of Woden Law. Two camps are particularly impressive and are represented by enclosing ramparts and ditches, with protective traverses in front of the gateways. Access is *via* a stile, sited 200m south of Pennymuir Hall, from the modern road which marks the line of Roman *Dere Street*.

18 Siller Holes, West Linton; NT 145 533

Situated beside a modern lane which follows the former line of the strategic Roman road from Carlisle to the Forth, Siller Holes is a pitted and scarred hill side from which lead, and perhaps silver, have been extracted since at least the 14th century. Beads found in one of the West

Water *cists* (*see below*) may contain lead from this site.

Although the workings are not open to the public, they may be viewed from the path which is one of a network which radiates from West Linton Village.

19   The Meldon Valley, Lyne and Peebles; NT 212 429

The valley of the Meldon Burn contains picnic sites, information on archaeology and wildlife, parking and toilet facilities. Spectacular views of the surrounding countryside can be obtained from summits of Black Meldon and White Meldon, both of which are crowned by *Iron Age hillforts*. *Bronze Age burial cairns* are also a feature of the district, and prehistoric farmsteads occupy sites on the lower slopes.

20   Trimontium Exhibition, Market Square, Melrose; NT 547 339

Finds, reconstructions and other information about the Roman military complex at *Trimontium* (Newstead) and the *hillfort* on Eildon North Hill are presented here. Guided walks around the Roman site are also available in season.

21   Prehistoric cemetery, Golf Course, West Linton; NT 138 518

A *Bronze Age cist* cemetery from nearby West Water Reservoir has been reconstructed on a knoll beside the modern lane which marks the former Roman

strategic road from Carlisle to the Forth. Foot access is *via* the old Roman road, which forms part of a network of local walks from West Linton Village.

22   Wilton Lodge Museum, Hawick; NT 493 145

The museum holds archaeological and zoological collections, with particular reference to the Hawick area and Teviotdale.

23   Early Christian tombstone, Yarrow; NT 3481 2745

The Yarrow Stone dates from the 5th century AD and records the burials of princes Nudus and Dumnogenus, sons of Liberalis. The stone now stands in a small enclosure beside the farm lane a short way from the public road.

Index

Field Notes

Field Notes